Contents

i

Contents

Punchouts

Name _____

Words with *sh*, *th*, or *wh*

Circle the word that makes sense in the sentence. Write the word.

_____

1. _____ are your friends?

   When   Who

_____

2. Is _____ your pet bird?

   that   then

_____

3. See the _____ !

   ship   shut

_____

4. Is _____ your paper?

   them   this

Name _____

Words with *sh*, *th*, or *wh*

 Circle the word that names the picture.
Write the word.

1.

ship
fish

_____

- -

_____

2.

path
math

_____

- -

_____

3.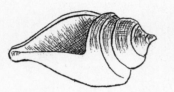

shed
shell

_____

- -

_____

4.

whisk
which

_____

- -

_____

5.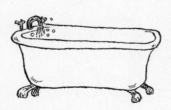

bath
with

_____

- -

_____

6.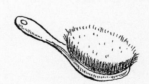

dish
brush

_____

- -

_____

Name _____

Words with *ch* or *tch*

Read the story. Write each **ch** or **tch** word in dark print below the picture it names.

Look at Jan **pitch.**
Mitch can **catch.**
Rich fell on a **branch.**
His **chin** got a scratch.

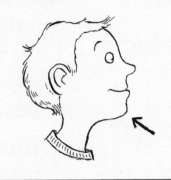

1. _____

2. _____

3. _____

4. _____

Name _____

Words with *ch* or *tch*

 Circle the word that makes sense in each sentence.
Write the word.

_____

1. Let's eat _____ .

latch
lunch

_____

2. I can _____ on the lamp.

switch
stitch

_____

3. You can sit on the _____ .

bench
batch

_____

4. Did you _____ this fish?

cast
catch

_____

5. I got a big _____ !

bunch
much

Name _____

Words to Know

Write a word from the box to complete each sentence.

1. My hat is too _____ .

   _____

2. I need more _____ in my hat!

   _____

3. These hats are too _____ .

   _____

4. When I _____ more, these hats will fit.

   _____

5. That hat is too _____ .

   _____

6. This other hat is just _____ .

| small |
| smell |

| room |
| these |

| more |
| long |

| grow |
| grass |

| other |
| light |

| right |
| room |

Name _____

Words to Know

 Read each pair of sentences. Draw a picture to go with them.

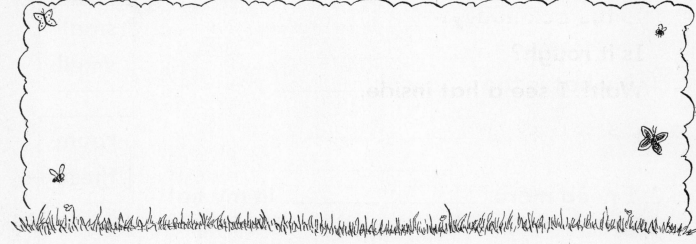

These flowers are small.
There is room to grow more!

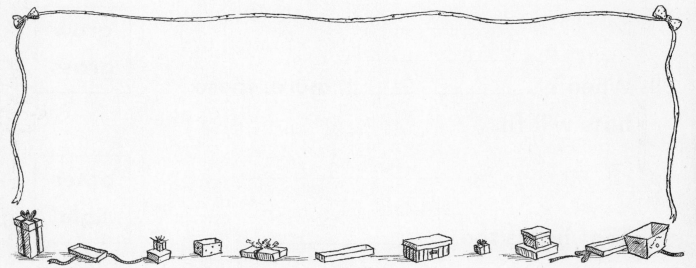

Here is a long, light box.
This other box is just right.

What's Inside?

Read the story. Draw a picture to show what happens.

What did Pam hide inside that plain box?

Is the box heavy?

Is it rough?

Wait! I see a hat inside.

It's a fancy hat!

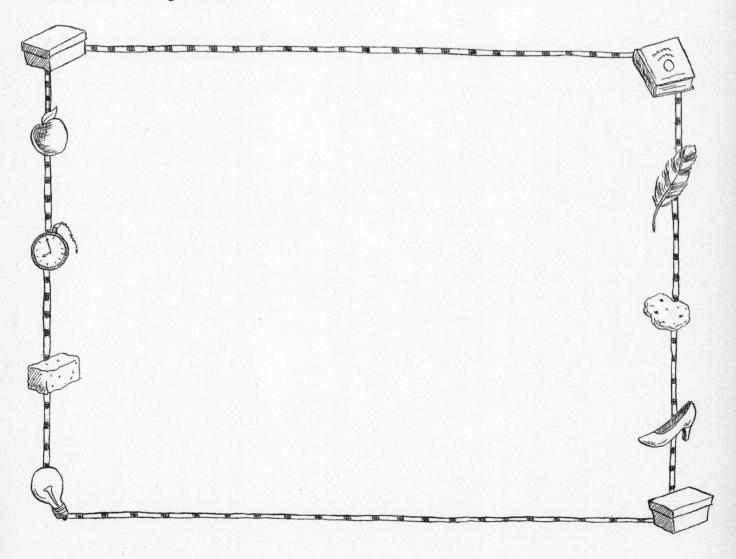

Theme 5: **Home Sweet Home**   **7**

Name _____

Retell the Story!

✂ Cut out and paste the sentences in order.
Read them to retell **Moving Day.**

1.

2.

3.

4.

| The next shells are too big and too small. | The crab finds a shell that is just right. |
| Many other shells will not do. | The crab's shell is snug. |

Name _____

Opposites!

Read each word. Circle its opposite in the box.

1. **first**

| last | see | eat |

2. **cold**

| pass | hot | here |

3. **go**

| grow | run | stop |

4. **down**

| upon | here | up |

5. **to**

| from | do | four |

6. **big**

| light | small | right |

7. **more**

| big | long | less |

8. **come**

| go | catch | trip |

Name _____

Exclamations

Read each pair of sentences. Circle the exclamation.

1. **Look at these shells!**

   Are these shells for Chip?

2. **She can hold them.**

   I want to hold them!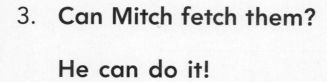

3. **Can Mitch fetch them?**

   He can do it!

4. **Look at this bunch!**

   I like the green batch.

5. **What a long shell it is!**

   The blue shell is small.

14 Theme 5: **Home Sweet Home**

Name _____

Long *a*

Circle the word that names each picture.

Write the word.

1.

gave
lace
gate

_____

2.

game
face
fake

_____

3.

cape
trace
cage

_____

4.

cage
cake
safe

_____

5.

skate
scale
lake

_____

6.

frame
rake
race

_____

Theme 5: **Home Sweet Home**   **19**

Name _____

Long *a*

Read the sentences. Write each word in dark print below the picture it names.

We swim in the **lake**.

We **skate** on the path.

Kate and I play a **game**.

We eat a **plate** of fish.

1.

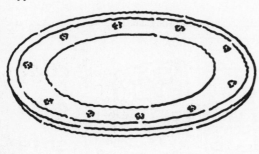

_____

- - - - - - - - - - - - - - -

_____

2.

_____

- - - - - - - - - - - - - - -

_____

3.

_____

- - - - - - - - - - - - - - -

_____

4.

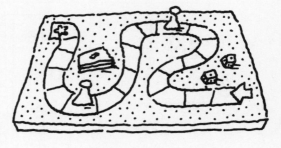

_____

- - - - - - - - - - - - - - -

_____

Ends with *nd*, *ng*, or *nk*

Circle the word that makes sense in each sentence. Write the word.

_____

1. The bird has hurt its _____ .

   sing   wing

_____

2. It can't fly in the _____ .

   wind   bend

_____

3. I _____ I can help.

   pink   think

_____

4. It will take a _____ time.

   ring   long

_____

5. But the bird will _____ .

   mend   lend

Name _____

Words to Know

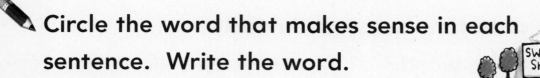

Circle the word that makes sense in each
sentence. Write the word.

1. How could you see all the places

   _____

   -

   in the _____ ?

   world   many

   _____

   -

2. You _____ look at a map.

   cold   could

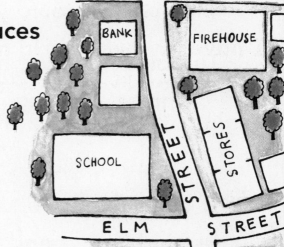

   _____

   -

3. Your own _____ is over here.

   house   how

   _____

   - - - - - - - - - - - - -

4. _____ take a look at the world!

   So   Some

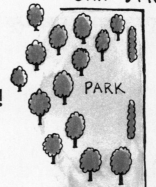

Name _____

Words to Know

Read the story, and do what it tells you to do.

    Dan said, "Could you make a world map?
I have my own world map at my house.
Would you like to come over and see it?"

Draw your own world map. Write sentences
to tell how you did it.

_____

_____

_____

Name _____

Story Words

✏ Read the story. Use words from the box to complete the story.

Word Bank

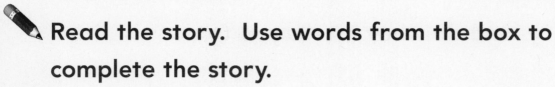

| ball | town | countries | Earth | giant |

We live on _____ . Earth looks

like a _____ green and blue

_____ . All the people on Earth have

special places to live. These places are called

_____ . In my country,

I live in a small _____ on a long street.

Name _____

Why We Need Maps

Look at the pictures, and answer the questions
below. Circle the answer.

Picture 1   Picture 2

1. In Picture 1, how do the people   sad   glad
   look?

2. In Picture 1, do they know where   yes   no
   they are?

3. How do the people look in   sad   glad
   Picture 2?

4. Did the people get help?   yes   no

Write a sentence to tell one thing maps can do.

_____

_____

_____

_____

Name _____

The Long *a* Sound

Word Bank

make came take name gave game

✏️ **Write three words from the box that rhyme.**

_____   _____   _____

_____   _____   _____

Write two words from the box that rhyme.

_____   _____

_____   _____

Write the word from the box that has not been used.

_____

_____

Name _____

Long *i*

Color the pictures whose names have the long i sound.

1.

2.

3.

4.

5.

6.

7.

8.

9.

Name _____

Long *i*

Name each picture. Use the letters in the box to write the word.

| e i p z r |

_____

----- ----- ----- -----

1. ___ ___ ___ ___ ___

| n v i e |

_____

----- ----- -----

2. ___ ___ ___ ___

| i m s e l |

_____

----- ----- ----- -----

3. ___ ___ ___ ___ ___

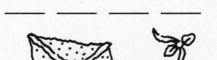

| t k i e |

_____

----- ----- -----

4. ___ ___ ___ ___

| e b i k |

_____

----- ----- -----

5. ___ ___ ___ ___

| l d i s e |

_____

----- ----- ----- ----- -----

6. ___ ___ ___ ___ ___

34   Theme 5: **Home Sweet Home**

Words to Know

Read each story. Draw a picture to show what happens.

Let's give our dog a bath.

That was a good thing to do!

Her little bird can't fly yet.

She will try to help it.

Name _____

Wet! Wet! Wet!

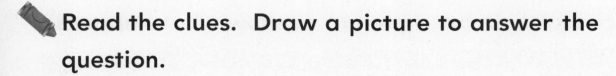 Read the clues. Draw a picture to answer the question.

It's raining today. It's perfect weather for us. Where are you? I'm convinced you are here. There isn't anywhere I haven't looked. Good news! There you are! That was easy! You look beautiful to me!

What do you think it is?

Name _____

What Happened?

Draw the beginning, middle, and end of **The Kite.** Write about the story.

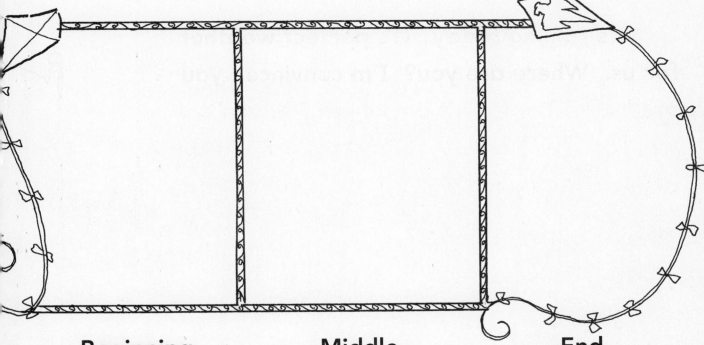

| Beginning | Middle | End |

_____

_____

_____

_____

_____

_____

Name _____

The Long *i* Sound

Color the kites whose words have the long i sound.

Spelling Words

| like | five | ride | nine | time | kite |

Write the Spelling Words from the kites you colored.

1. _____

2. _____

3. _____

4. _____

5. _____

6. _____

Theme 5: **Home Sweet Home**   **43**

Name _____

Words with *-ing*

 Add **-ing** to the base words.
Write the new words.

┌─ - - - - - - - - ─┐
│   **-ing**   │
└─ - - - - - - - - ─┘

walk

_____

- - - - - - - - - - - - - - - - - - -

_____

do

_____

- - - - - - - - - - - - - - - - - - -

_____

call

_____

- - - - - - - - - - - - - - - - - - -

_____

fly

_____

- - - - - - - - - - - - - - - - - - -

_____

Write a sentence using one of the words you wrote.

_____

- -

_____

_____

- -

_____

Using *I* or *Me*

Read each sentence. Circle the word that completes the sentence, and write it on the line.

1. _____ have a big family.

    I   Me

2. Give _____ the can.

    me   I

3. My mother and _____ went to the lake.

    me   I

4. Can you come with _____ ?

    I   me

Write a sentence using **I** or **me**.

_____

_____

Name _____

Spelling Spree

 Circle and write the hidden Spelling Word.

Spelling Words

| like | five | ride | nine | time | kite |

1. eninep

_____

- - - - - - - - - - -

_____

2. timeur

_____

- - - - - - - - - - -

_____

3. cfiveg

_____

- - - - - - - - - - -

_____

 Proofread each sentence. Circle each Spelling Word that is wrong, and write it correctly.

4. I like to rid my bike.

_____

- - - - - - - - - - -

_____

5. I like to fly my cit.

_____

- - - - - - - - - - -

_____

6. Do you lik these things, too?

_____

- - - - - - - - - - -

_____

Name _____

Phonics

Now use what you have learned about taking tests. Your teacher will tell you what to do. This practice will help you when you take this kind of test.

1   grab   sack   ship   rush
       ○   ○   ○   ○

2   thin   shop   when   tell
       ○   ○   ○   ○

3   shop   cat   dish   chop
       ○   ○   ○   ○

Name _____

Phonics continued

4   back   gave   kite   bug
         ○   ○   ○   ○

5   hill   name   like   hid
         ○   ○   ○   ○

6   take   pad   gap   side
         ○   ○   ○   ○

Name _____

Spelling Review

Name each picture. Write a Spelling Word that has the same vowel sound.

shell

fish

chop

much

gave

kite

1. _____

2. _____

Write two Spelling Words that have **ch**.

3. _____

4. _____

Write two Spelling Words that have **sh**.

5. _____

6. _____

Theme 5: **Home Sweet Home**   **51**

Name _____

Spelling Spree

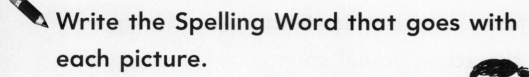 Write the Spelling Word that goes with each picture.

fish

chop

make

like

name

ride

_____
- - - - - - - - - - - - - - - - - -

1. I have on a _____ tag.

_____
- - - - - - - - - - - - - - - - - -

2. He will _____ it down.

_____
- - - - - - - - - - - - - - - - - -

3. The _____ can see a bug.

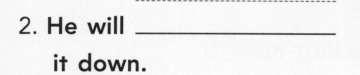 Proofread each sentence. Circle each Spelling Word that is wrong, and write it correctly.

_____
- - - - - - - - - - - - - - - - - -

4. Let the kite ried on the wind.

_____
- - - - - - - - - - - - - - - - - -

5. Mak the kite go up, up, up!

_____
- - - - - - - - - - - - - - - - - -

6. It can fly lik a bird.

Name _____

Long *o*

Circle the word that goes with each picture, and write it on the line.

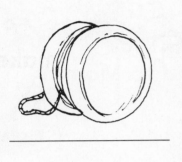

yo-yo

fish

yam

1. _____

bake

broke

clock

2. _____

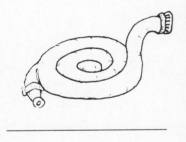

hope

mug

hose

3. _____

cane

cone

drum

4. _____

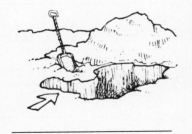

hole

home

cluck

5. _____

rose

room

robe

6. _____

Name _____

Long *o*

Circle and write the word that completes each sentence.

_____

- - - - - - - - - - - - - - - -

1. "Can we _____ to Jo's?" I said to Mom.

    go   not

_____

- - - - - - - - - - - - - - - - - - - -

2. My mom _____ me to Jo's house.

    hope   drove

_____

- - - - - - - - - - - - - - -

3. We can fix eggs on Jo's play _____ .

    froze   stove

_____

- - - - - - - - - - - - - - - - -

4. "Let's get a _____ for that vase," I said.

    rose   joke

_____

- - - - - - - - - - - - - - -

5. We wet the grass with the _____ .

    stone   hose

Name _____

Long u

Use the letters in the box to write the word
that goes with each picture.

etbu

1. ___ ___ ___ ___

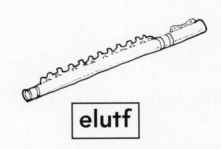

utec

2. ___ ___ ___ ___

heug

3. ___ ___ ___ ___

elutf

4. ___ ___ ___ ___

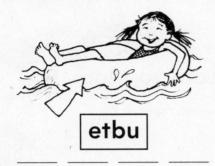

ulme

5. ___ ___ ___ ___

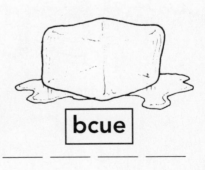

bcue

6. ___ ___ ___ ___

Name _____

Long *u*

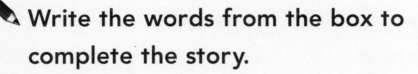

Write the words from the box to complete the story.

Word Bank

flute   huge   cute   mule   tune

_____

The girl plays a _____ on the

_____ . The _____

kicks its legs. The mule gives the girl a

_____ kiss. It's so _____ !

Ends with *ft*, *lk*, or *nt*

Circle the word that makes sense in the sentence. Write the word.

_____

1. An _____ gets in Kent's bag.

      ant   bent

_____

2. Kent and the ant have hot dogs and _____ .

     sulk   milk

_____

3. They have a _____ bed.

     soft   lift

_____

4. Kent and the ant _____ the camp.

     gift   left

_____

5. The ant _____ the trip with Kent!

     spent   cent

Name _____

Words to Know

Make sentences. Write the words from each box in the correct order. Add a period at the end of the sentence.

> a bird one by I found morning house my

_____

- -

_____

> shout my to I out dad

_____

- -

_____

> how climb to nest Show the me to

_____

- -

_____

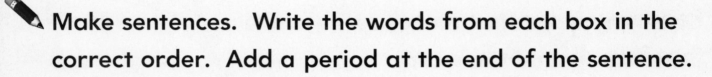

58   Theme 6: **Animal Adventures**

Name _____

Words to Know

Read each pair of sentences. Circle the sentence that tells about the picture.

You do not have to shout!

I know that girl.

I will show you how to ride.

I ate too much!

In the morning, I climb out of bed fast.

Here is my mother.

My room is big.

I found a dime by the swing.

Story Vocabulary

Read the story. Use the box to help you find and circle some words from **The Sleeping Pig.**

Word Bank

begfor

began

celebrate

coyote

cricket

howl

rabbit

tail

watermelon

It was fall, so Cricket said, "Let's celebrate!" Coyote let out a howl. Rabbit jumped and twitched his tail up and down.

Then they began to eat a huge watermelon!

Draw a picture to go with the story.

Name _____

Who Tried to Wake Up Mrs. Pig?

Draw one animal that helped Celina.

Write about what that animal did.

_____

- -

_____

_____

- -

_____

_____

- -

_____

Name _____

Problems, Problems

Write two problems the family has in **The Kite**. In the box, draw or write how the problems were solved.

Problems

_____

- -

_____

_____

- -

_____

_____

- -

_____

Solutions

Name _____

List Your Reasons

Use this page to plan how to convince a friend that you should have a pet.

What kind of pet do you want?

_____
- -
_____

Write why you should get that pet.

_____
- -
_____
_____
- -
_____
_____
- -
_____

Read what you wrote to a friend. What can you add?

_____
- -
_____
_____
- -
_____

Name _____

Revising Your Description

 Put a check next to the sentences that tell about your writing.

Superstar

☐ I told the reader what I am describing.

☐ My description tells how something looks, feels, sounds, tastes, and smells.

☐ My description uses exact words.

☐ My description makes a clear picture for the reader.

Rising Star

☐ I need to tell what I am describing.

☐ I need to add words that tell how something looks, feels, sounds, tastes, and smells.

☐ I could change some of my words to more exact words.

☐ I could make a clearer picture for the reader.

Name _____

Long *e*

Read the story. Circle all the words with the long e sound.

My friend Pete came to me with a plan. We can have a play. These friends can be in it — Steve, Rose, and Mel. The theme of our play can be "Friends."

Draw a picture to go along with the story.

Name _____

Words with *ee, ea*

Read each word. If the word has long **e** spelled **ea**, write it under **peach**. If the word has long **e** spelled **ee**, write it under **jeep**.

Word Bank

bean	sheep	seat	beep
keep	eat	teeth	beach

peach

jeep

_____

1. _____

_____

3. _____

_____

5. _____

_____

7. _____

_____

2. _____

_____

4. _____

_____

6. _____

_____

8. _____

Name _____

Words with *ee*, *ea*

Read each sentence. Write each word in dark print below the picture it names.

A **bee** stung a dog.
The dog broke its **leash**.
The dog ran to a **tree**.
The dog ate a **peach**.

1. _____

2. _____

3. _____

4. _____

Name _____

Words to Know

Write the words that name things in a house in the house shape. Write the words that name things that live in a barn in the barn shape.

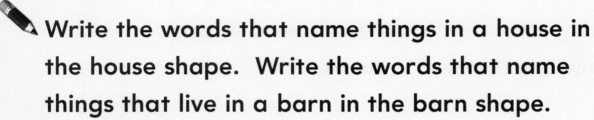

Word Bank

cow	table	now	door
there	through	horse	wall

Write the rest of the words.

_____

_____

Name _____

Words to Know

Write a word from the box to complete each sentence in the story.

Word Bank

table	there	horse	through	wall

_____

1. The _____ walked through the door.

2. The cow walked _____ the door.

3. The horse sat at the _____ .

4. The cow sat by the _____ .

5. Now _____ was a funny picture!

Name _____

EEK! Look at These Words!

Write a word from the box that goes with each picture.

Word Bank

| marched | elephant | tangled |
| dancing | barn | mouse |

1. _____

2. _____

3. _____

4. _____

5. _____

6. _____

What's It All About?

Read each sentence. Then draw a line from the sentence to the picture that completes it.

1. The cat knocked over a

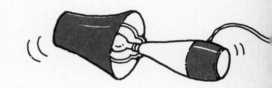

2. The dog broke a

3. The hog ate

4. The sheep got tangled in

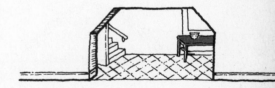

5. The hen was laying eggs on the

6. The elephant went in through the

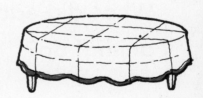

Details from the Story

Write about two characters from **EEK! There's a Mouse in the House.**

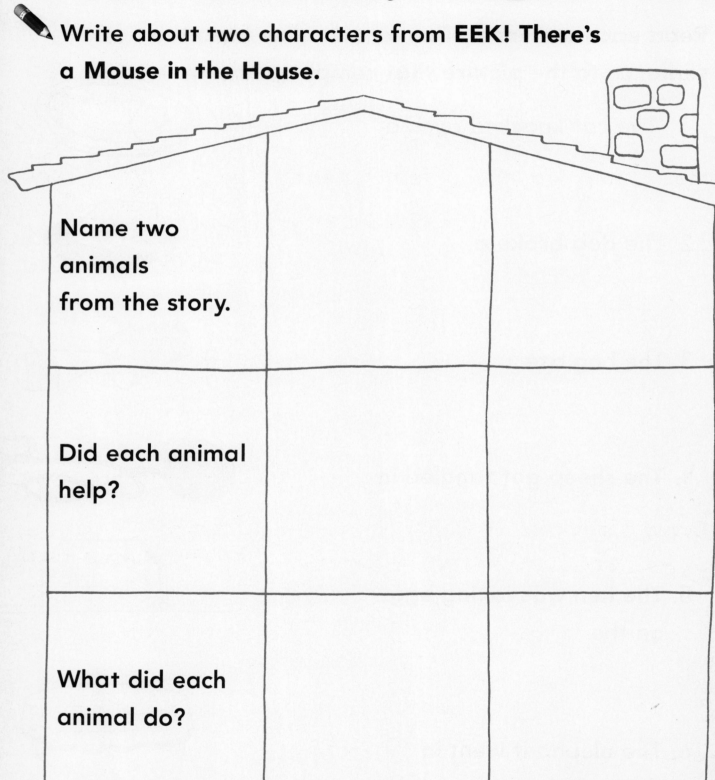

Name two animals from the story.		
Did each animal help?		
What did each animal do?		

Name _____

The Long *e* Sound

Write each word from the box under the word with the same long e spelling.

Spelling Words

| me | see | mean | feet | eat | he |

| we | meet | treat |

1. _____   2. _____   3. _____

4. _____   5. _____   6. _____

Draw a silly picture to match the silly sentence.

He sees mean beans that eat feet.

Name _____

Rhyme Time!

Read each word. Write each word from the box under the rhyming word.

Word Bank

mole	fake	three
we	hole	take
wake	me	role

cake   pole   he

_____ _____ _____

_____ _____ _____

_____ _____ _____

Name _____

Naming Words

Read each sentence. Circle the naming word and draw a picture of it.

1. Here is a green vase.

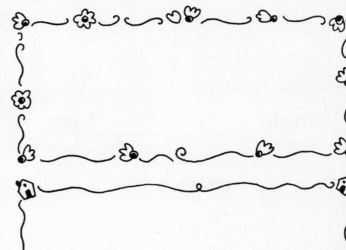

2. That house is small.

3. Where is my sled?

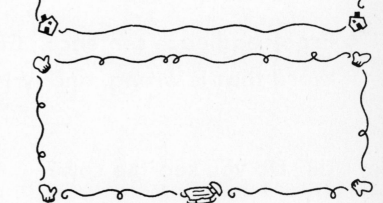

Use one of the circled words in a sentence.

_____

- -

_____

_____

- -

_____

Name _____

Spelling Spree

 Write the Spelling Word for each clue.

same as I

_____

----

1. _____

not nice   him

_____   _____

-------------------------   -------------------------

2. _____   3. _____

Spelling Words
me
see
mean
feet
eat
he

 Proofread each sentence. Circle each Spelling
Word that is wrong, and write it correctly.

_____

----

4. Do you sea the cow?   _____

_____

----

5. It has big fete.   _____

_____

----

6. It likes to eet grass.   _____

Name _____

What Happened?

Read each question about **EEK! There's a Mouse in the House**. Write your answer in a complete sentence.

1. What was the first animal that came in the house?

_____

_____

_____

_____

2. How do you think it got in the house?

_____

_____

_____

_____

3. Why did the girl think the elephant could get rid of all the other animals?

_____

_____

Name _____

Words with *ai* or *ay*

 Circle the word that names each picture, and write it on the line.

1.

paint   rain   day

1. _____

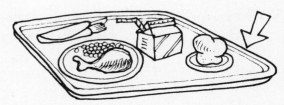

bay   tail   tray

2. _____

stain   hay   ray

3. _____

sail   pail   day

4. _____

clay   stay   wait

5. _____

spray   train   braid

6. _____

Name _____

Words with *ai* or *ay*

Read the words in the box. Then write each word under the word with the same spelling for the long **a** sound.

train

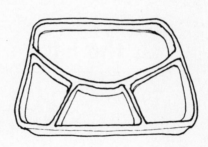

tray

1. _____

2. _____

3. _____

4. _____

5. _____

6. _____

7. _____

8. _____

Name _____

Words to Know

Read each pair of sentences. Circle the sentence that tells about the picture.

1. **Even**ing is here when the sun goes down.

   The **h**orse climbs the hill.

2. The **bi**rd **goes** in its nest.

   The for**est ha**s been a home to many animals.

3. It is not **far** to the lake.

   The animal is hungry.

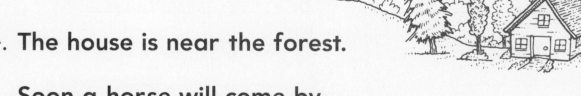

4. The house is near the forest.

   Soon a horse will come by.

Name _____

Words to Know

Read each word in the first list. Draw a line to
its opposite.

1. evening   full

2. near   morning

3. hungry   far

4. goes   comes

Have you ever been in a forest? Soon you will read
about one. Write about what you think may
live there.

_____

_____

_____

_____

_____

Name _____

Rain Forest Adventure

 Circle the word that names each picture.

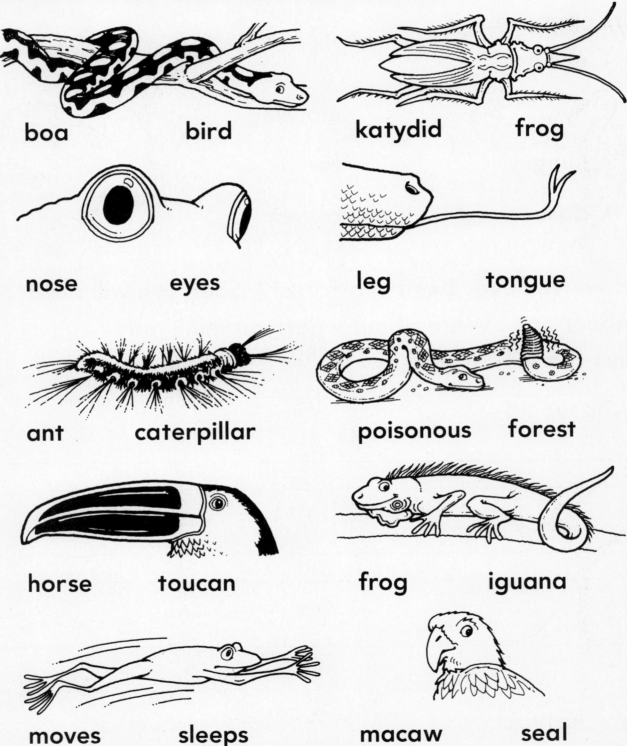

boa bird	katydid frog
nose eyes	leg tongue
ant caterpillar	poisonous forest
horse toucan	frog iguana
moves sleeps	macaw seal

Who's on the Menu?

Color the picture that answers each question.

What does the red-eyed tree frog eat?

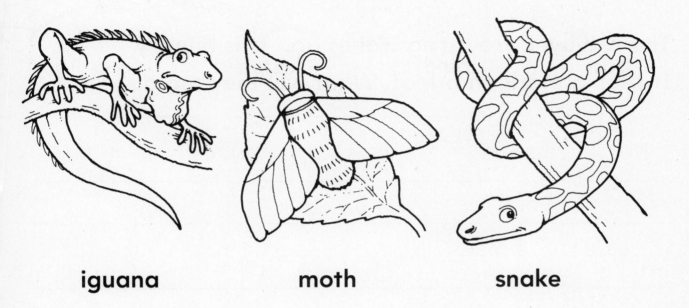

iguana   moth   snake

Who would eat the red-eyed tree frog?

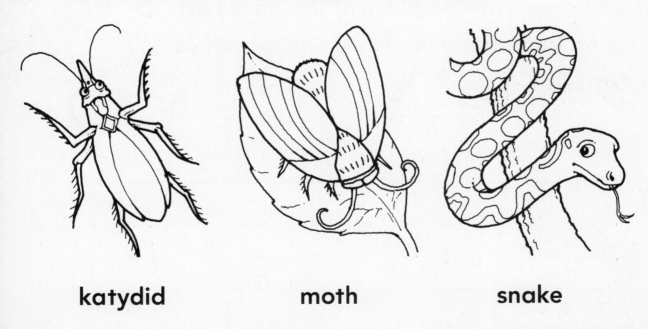

katydid   moth   snake

Name _____

What Happens Next?

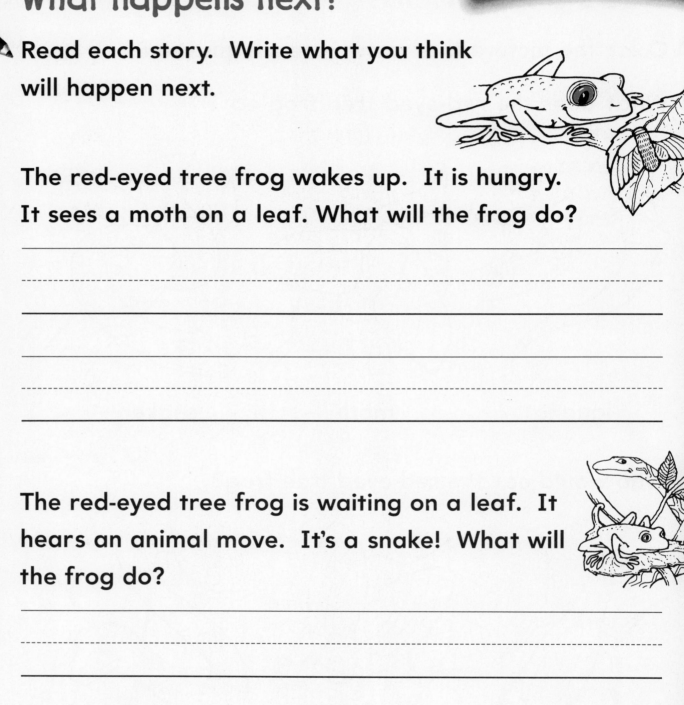

Read each story. Write what you think
will happen next.

The red-eyed tree frog wakes up. It is hungry.
It sees a moth on a leaf. What will the frog do?

_____

- -

_____

- -

_____

The red-eyed tree frog is waiting on a leaf. It
hears an animal move. It's a snake! What will
the frog do?

_____

- -

_____

- -

_____

Name _____

Sum It Up!

Think about the story **The Sleeping Pig**.

Write a summary of it.

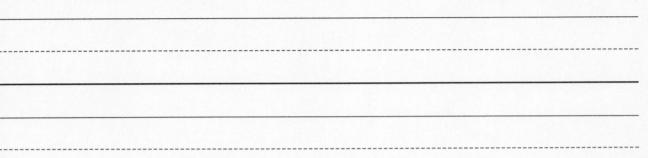

This story is about

_____

_____

_____

_____

_____

_____

_____

_____

Read what you wrote to a friend.

Name _____

Filling in the Blank

Now use what you have learned about taking tests. Answer these fill-in-the-blank questions about **Eek! There's a Mouse in the House.** Look back at the story if you need to. This practice will help you when you take this kind of test.

Read each sentence. Fill in the circle next to the best answer.

1 The girl would like the _____ to chase the rat.

- ○ dog
- ○ cat
- ○ cow

2 The hog _____ but does not chase the dog.

- ○ hops with a mop
- ○ cracks a dish
- ○ eats the cake

Name _____

Filling in the Blank continued

3 When the hen comes in, it _____.

   ○ lays eggs on the table

   ○ gets tangled up

   ○ mops up a mess

4 The _____ comes in from the stable.

   ○ **elephant**

   ○ **sheep**

   ○ **horse**

5 At the end of the story, the _____ is in the house with the mouse.

   ○ **cat**

   ○ **elephant**

   ○ **cow**

Name _____

Spelling Review

Write a Spelling Word next to each number.

Spelling Words

| go | home | me | mean | feet | stay |

1. _____

2. _____

3. _____

4. _____

5. _____

6. _____

Color the mice green next to the
long **e** words.
Color the mice brown next to the
long **a** words.
Color the mice red next to the
long **o** words.

Name _____

Spelling Spree

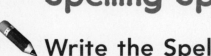 Write the Spelling Word that makes sense in each sentence.

Spelling Words

| day | nose | home | eat | feet | play |

1. My friend and I take a walk every
_____

_____ .

2. We jump and _____ in the mud.

3. We splash mud with our _____ .

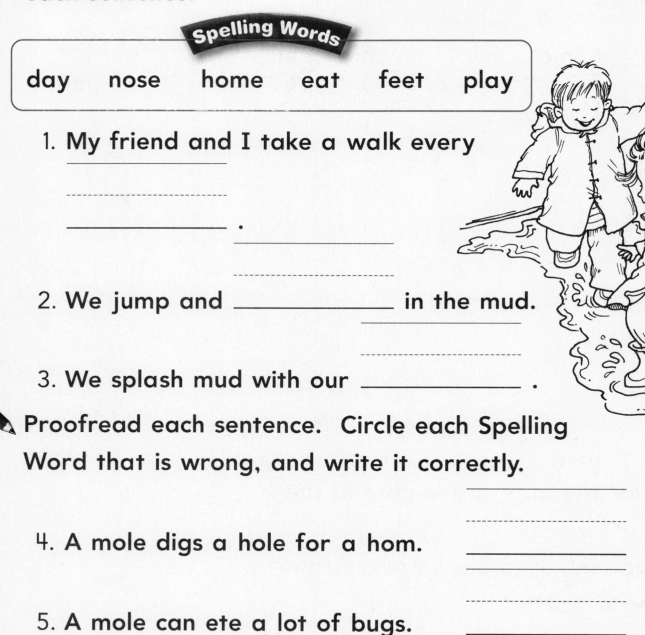 Proofread each sentence. Circle each Spelling Word that is wrong, and write it correctly.

4. A mole digs a hole for a hom.   _____

5. A mole can ete a lot of bugs.   _____

6. It has to find bugs with its nos.   _____

Name _____

Words with *oa* and *ow*

Write two words from the box to complete each sentence.

1. I see a _____ in the _____.

2. I see a _____ in a _____.

3. I see a _____ in the _____.

Name _____

Words with *oa* and *ow*

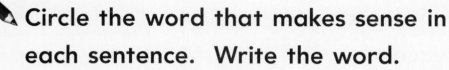 Circle the word that makes sense in each sentence. Write the word.

_____

1. "Sh! Go _____ ," said Fred.

      slow   grow

_____

2. "I know the _____ will hop," said Sue.

      goat   toad

_____

3. "Now, _____ me where it will go, Sue."

      show   glow

_____

4. "Look! See the toad hop up the _____ ."

      road   boat

Words to Know

Fold a piece of paper in half to make a book.

Cut and paste the story parts on the pages in order.

Write your own ending on the last page.

"Do I go this way or that way?" asked Toad.

"I can look at the map again," said Al.

"Look for Big Lake Road."

"We must both look for the road," said Toad.

"Pull the wheel hard so you don't hit that

hole!" said Al. "The map is gone, but there

is the lake!"

This Way or That Way?

"I want to go to the lake," said Al.

"Let's go, but it's my turn to drive,"

said Toad.

Name _____

Words to Know

Read the story. Find and circle the words
from the box in the story.

Word Bank

again	both	gone	or
want	turn	hard	

The cat, the dog, and the bee want to
play tag. The cat tags the bee. Now it's the
bee's turn, but where has the bee gone? Will
the bee tag the cat or the dog? It's hard
to do, but the bee tags both the cat and
the dog. Then the bee is gone again.

Draw a picture to show what happened.

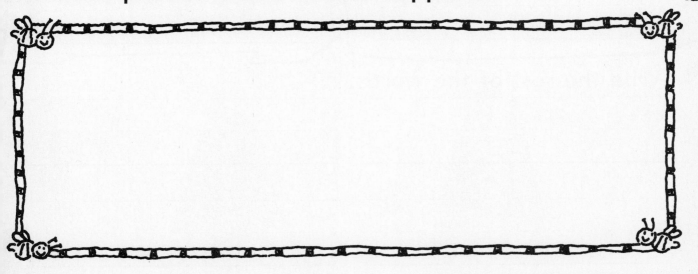

Name _____

Sort It Out!

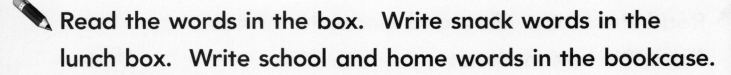 Read the words in the box. Write snack words in the lunch box. Write school and home words in the bookcase.

Word Bank

agree	books	candy bars	crayons	fault
food	hoptoad	lemonade	share	toys

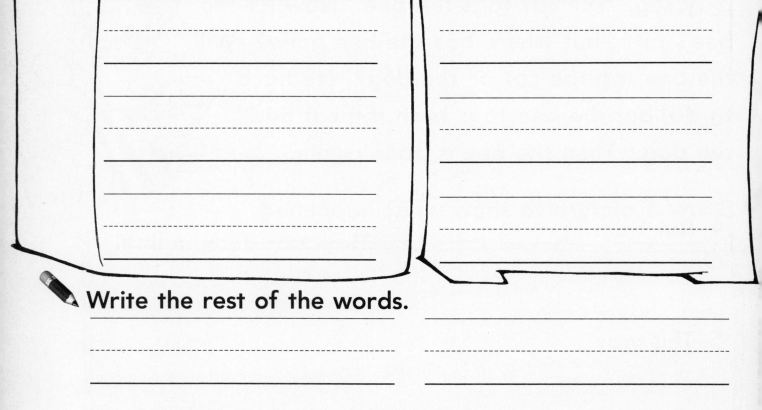

Write the rest of the words.

Name _____

Words to Know

Write a word from the box to complete each sentence.

_____

----

1. I am not _____ of the big, tall dog that looks like a bear.

_____

----

2. He can _____ me.

_____

----

3. I don't have _____ food.

_____

----

4. But I can give him _____ .

_____

----

5. This was a good _____ .

_____

----

6. Now _____ of the water is gone!

Name _____

A Ride to the Top

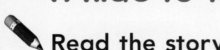 Read the story. Then answer the question.

This building is in the city. The building is so tall it looks like the top of it disappears! But I don't let it scare me. The friendly man meets us. He tells us not to worry. We take the elevator to the top. We can see the library and the park from up here!

Where are the people?

_____

_____

_____

_____

The Vowel Sound in *book*

Write a word from the box to complete each sentence.

Spelling Words

look
book
took
good
foot
cook

1. The cook hurt his _____ .

2. The _____ will rest his foot.

3. The cook will read a _____ .

4. The cook _____ a nap.

5. Now _____ , his foot is fine.

6. It will be a _____ day.

Name _____

Many Meanings

 Write the word from the box that completes both
sentences in each pair.

Word Bank

fall	back	left	set

1. I ____ my book at home.   _____

   I write with my ____ hand.   _____

2. We rake the leaves in the ____.   _____

   I like to ____ into the pile of leaves.   _____

3. I have an itch on my ____.   _____

   We will send the box ____ to you.   _____

4. I have a ____ of books on animals.   _____

   Can you ____ that plate down here?   _____

Name _____

Name It!

Read the special naming words. Write a special naming word to go with each picture.

Word Bank

Main Street	Al's Pet Shop
Lost Lake	Redwood City

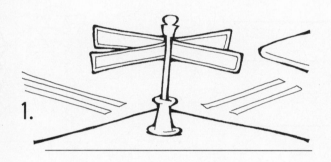

1. _____

- - - - - - - - - - - - - - - - - -

_____

2. _____

- - - - - - - - - - - - - - - - - -

_____

3. _____

- - - - - - - - - - - - - - - - - -

_____

4. _____

- - - - - - - - - - - - - - - - - -

_____

Spelling Spree

✏️ Write the missing letters to complete each Spelling Word. Write the word.

1. f __ __ t   _____

2. c __ __ k   _____

3. t __ __ k   _____

✏️ Proofread each sentence. Circle each spelling word that is wrong, and write it correctly.

4. Luk here.   _____

5. There is the bok.   _____

6. It is a gud book.   _____

Pig Knew What to Do

Finish each sentence with a word from the Word Bank. Write each word in the correct puzzle boxes.

1. Pig got a ___ pot.
2. He ___ in some glue.
3. He got a few boots, ___.
4. ___ the pot was hot.
5. The ___ was all set.
6. "___ can come eat," said Pig.

Word Bank

threw
You
too
new
Soon
soup

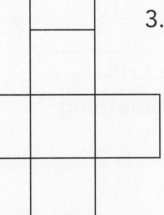

2.

4.

3.

1.

6.

5.

Name _____

A Ride on the Slide

Read the word at the top of the slide. Write new words as you go down the slide. The first one is done for you.

Change the **m** in **might** to **s**.

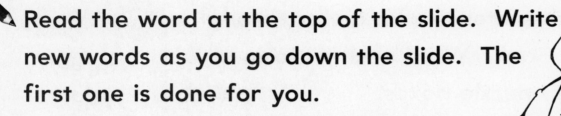

m i g h t
s i g h t

1. Change the **s** in **sight** to **r**.

2. Change the **r** in **right** to **n**.

3. Change the **n** in **night** to **t**.

4. Change the **t** in **tight** to **l**.

Change the **t** in **tie** to **p** to name something good to eat.

Name _____

Words to Know

Fold a piece of paper in half to make a book. Cut and paste the story parts on the pages in order.

Write your own ending on the last page.

Little Pig did not wear his boots. He left them under his bed. His old shoes get very wet in the rain.

A New House

Miss Pig wants a new house. Little Pig will start to build it.

Wet Little Pig gets a piece of cake from Miss Pig.

Name _____

Word Match

Draw a line from each naming word to the
word that can take its place. Write each word.

1.  **cats**

   She

2. **Mike**

   they

3.  **Ann**

   it

4.  **bat**

   he

Write the letter from each box to make a word that
answers the question.

_____

Who can play with Ann and Mike? _____

Name _____

Spelling Spree

 **Write the Spelling Word for
each clue.**

Spelling Words

| zoo | food | too | moon | room |

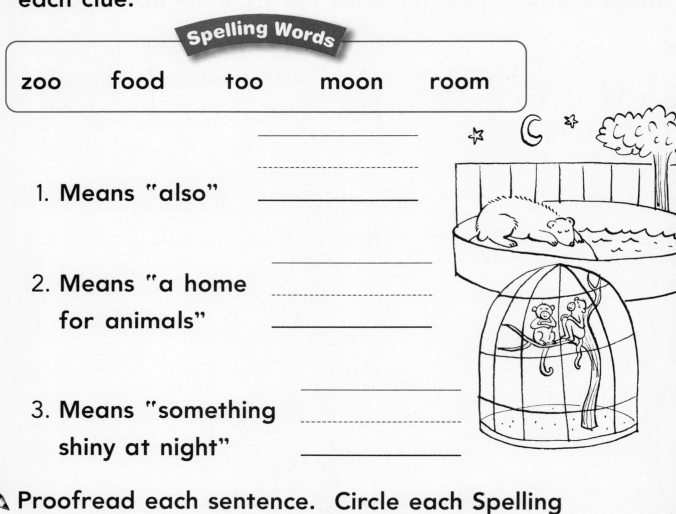

1. Means "also" _____

2. Means "a home
for animals" _____

3. Means "something
shiny at night" _____

 **Proofread each sentence. Circle each Spelling
Word that is wrong, and write it correctly.**

4. Look at that fod. _____

5. It is all over this rom. _____

Please Come!

Write words to finish the invitation.

Come to a Birthday Party!

_____

_____

Dear _____ ,

_____

Day: _____

_____

Time: _____

_____

Where: _____

_____

_____ is giving the party.

Name _____

Writing a Personal Response

Now use what you have learned about taking tests. Write your answer to the question. Then see how you might make your answer better. This practice will help you when you take this kind of test.

In the story **If You Give a Pig a Pancake**, the girl gives the pig a pancake. The pig wants more. Have you given something to someone who said they wanted more? Write about what you would say to that person.

_____

- -

_____

- -

_____

- -

_____

- -

_____

Name _____

Writing a Personal Response

continued

✏ Read the answer that you wrote on page 147. Check each box that tells about your answer.

☐ My sentences answer the question.

☐ My sentences tell what I think.

☐ My sentences have interesting details.

✏ If you did not check a box, you can make your answer better. Make your changes here.

_____

_____

_____

_____

_____

_____

Name _____

Spelling Review

Write the Spelling Words.

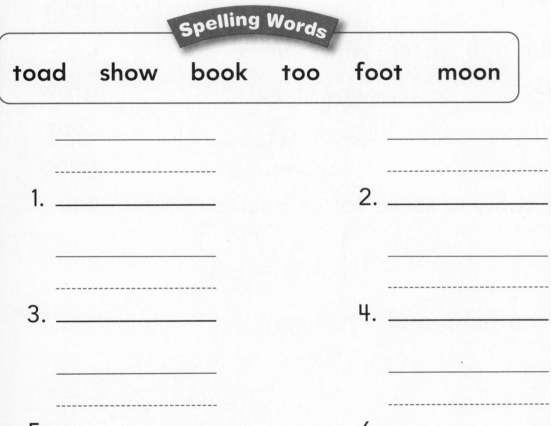

Spelling Words

| toad | show | book | too | foot | moon |

1. _____

2. _____

3. _____

4. _____

5. _____

6. _____

Circle the words with the long **o** sound.
Put a check by the words with the vowel
sound in **cool**.
Draw a smile by the words with the vowel
sound in **hook**.

Name _____

Spelling Spree

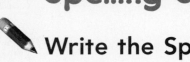 Write the Spelling Word that answers each question.

toad

look

grow

coat

good

zoo

1. With sun and water, what can a plant do?

   _____

   _____

2. Where can you see a lot of animals?

   _____

   _____

3. What can jump and eat bugs?

   _____

   _____

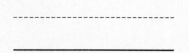

Proofread each sentence. Circle each Spelling Word that is wrong, and write it correctly.

4. Can you help me luk for my dog?

   _____

   _____

5. Boots is a gud dog.

   _____

6. He has spots on his cote.

   _____

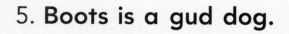

A Fine Time!

Circle and write the correct word to complete each sentence.

_____

1. Toad and Bear _____ by the pond.

            playing   played

_____

2. Ant _____ at the food.

            looked   looking

_____

3. "Why is Ant _____ at the food?" asked Toad.

            peeking   peeks

_____

4. "Ant _____ to eat!" said Bear.

            wanting   wants

Name _____

Words to Know

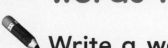 Write a word from the box to complete each sentence.

Word Bank

tiny	part	because	teacher	happy

1. Our _____ tells us about plants.

2. Plants grow _____ they get sun.

3. We draw each _____ of a plant.

4. It has little, _____ seeds.

5. We feel _____ drawing plants.

Name _____

Words to Know

Read each pair of sentences. Circle the
sentence that tells about the picture.

I feel happy when I
draw cars.

Tiny seeds are part of
this plant.

Plants grow because they
get water and sun.

Our teacher tells us
about frogs.

Name _____

Interesting Plants

Read each sentence Draw a line from the sentence to the picture it goes with.

There are many different types of plants.

1. Some plants have beautiful flowers.

2. Be careful of poisonous plants.

3. Some trees have long branches.

4. Acorns are nuts from the oak tree.

Name _____

A Forest Visit

▲ **Read the directions and write the answers.**

1. **Name three things that make their homes in the forest.**

   _____

   -

   _____

   -

   _____

   -

   _____

2. **Name one thing to be careful about in the forest.**

   _____

   -

   _____

   -

   _____

Name _____

Forest Life

Look at the picture. Write in the correct box the names of the things you see.

Animals	Plants

Name _____

Busy Times

Draw a line from each picture to the action word that goes with it. Write each action word.

1. _____

   eat _____

2. _____

   dig _____

3. _____

   swim _____

4. _____

   sit _____

5. _____

   fly _____

Spelling Spree

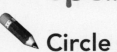 Circle and write the hidden Spelling Words.

 Spelling Words

| cup | cups | frog | frogs | tree | trees |

1. lcupfa _____

2. gtreec _____

3. rifrog _____

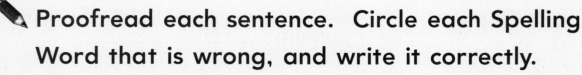 Proofread each sentence. Circle each Spelling
Word that is wrong, and write it correctly.

4. Birds live in the treas . _____

5. Frugs live in the pond. _____

6. I have two cps. _____

Name _____

My Learning Log

Write some facts about **The Forest**.

Draw pictures to go with the facts.

Animals

_____

- -

_____

- -

_____

- -

_____

Trees

_____

- -

_____

- -

_____

- -

_____

Name _____

Revising Your Research Report

 Check the sentences that tell about your research report.

Superstar

- [ ] I wrote facts that were interesting.
- [ ] I used at least two sources to get information about my topic.
- [ ] I wrote the facts in my own words.
- [ ] I included enough facts.
- [ ] I wrote the information in an order that makes sense.

Rising Star

- [ ] I could have written facts that were more interesting.
- [ ] I used only one source to get information about my topic.
- [ ] I did not always use my own words.
- [ ] I could have added more facts.
- [ ] Some of the information is not in an order that makes sense.

Name _____

A Hike in the Woods

Circle the word that makes sense in each sentence. Write the word.

_____
----

1. We hike _____ the trail.

   found   down

_____
----

2. We do not _____ .

   shout   now

_____
----

3. We see an _____ .

   owl   clown

_____
----

4. We see a _____ run by.

   flower   mouse

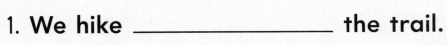
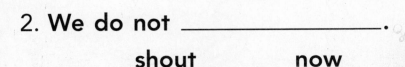
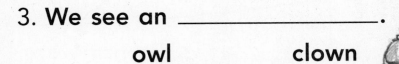

Name _____

Something Funny!

 Read the story. Circle the two-syllable words.

"Follow me," said Big Mouse to Little Mouse.

"Let's eat that oatmeal," said Big Mouse.

The mice ate. What a funny sight!

 Write the two-syllable words from the story.

1. _____

2. _____

3. _____

4. _____

Name _____

Words to Know

Fold a piece of paper in half to make a book.

Cut and paste the story parts on the pages in order.

Write your own ending on the last page.

1

Always warm up your arms and legs.
One, two, three, four.

2

Stretch your body.
Five, six, seven, eight.

3

Ready! Set! Go!

Theme 8: **Our Earth**   169

Name _____

Words to Know

Write a word from the box to complete each sentence.

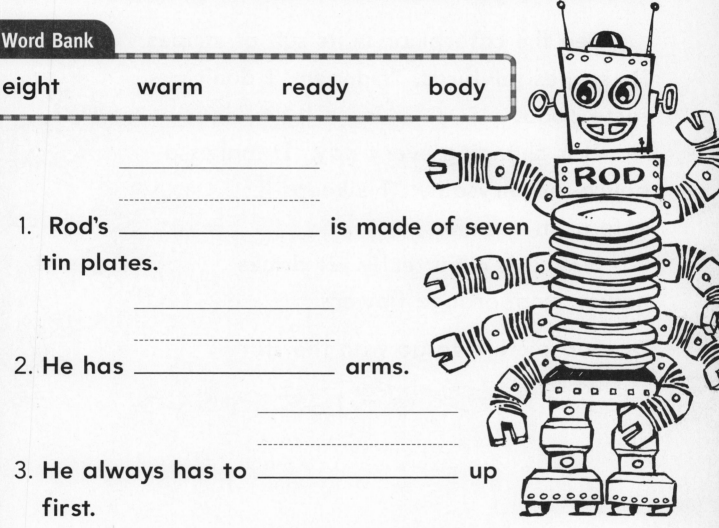

Word Bank

| eight | warm | ready | body |

_____

1. Rod's _____ is made of seven tin plates.

_____

2. He has _____ arms.

_____

3. He always has to _____ up first.

_____

4. Then he is _____ to pick up trash!

Name _____

Something to See

Read the story.

See the caterpillar in its suit of stripes. Its stripes tell birds, "Danger! I don't taste good!"

It is changing every day. It makes a pouch, or chrysalis. This keeps it safe from enemies.

Now it is a butterfly. It drinks nectar from orange flowers.

Draw a picture to go with the story.

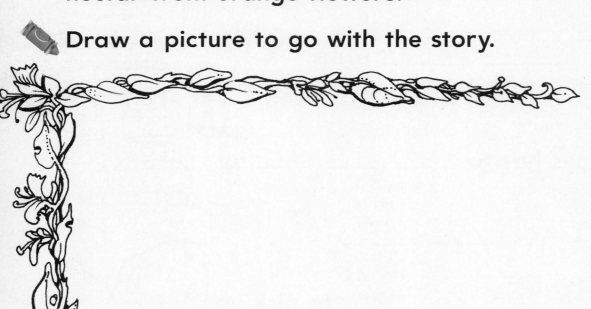

Name _____

Right Now!

Choose words from Box 1 and Box 2 to make four
sentences. Write the sentences.

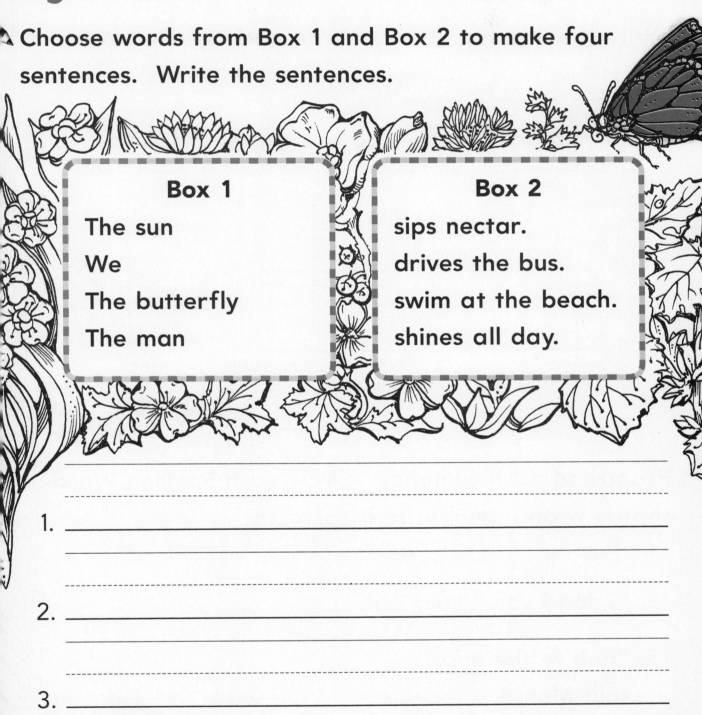

Box 1

The sun

We

The butterfly

The man

Box 2

sips nectar.

drives the bus.

swim at the beach.

shines all day.

1. _____

2. _____

3. _____

4. _____

Name _____

Spelling Spree

Write the missing letters. Write each Spelling Word.

Spelling Words

| cow | house | out | down | now | found |

1. d ___ ___ n _____

2. c ___ ___ _____

3. n ___ ___ _____

Proofread each sentence. Circle each Spelling Word that is wrong, and write it correctly.

4. "I fond you," said Cat. _____

5. "Run to the huse," said Mouse. _____

6. "Come owt!" said Cat. _____

Write About a Topic

◢ **Plan your paragraph.**

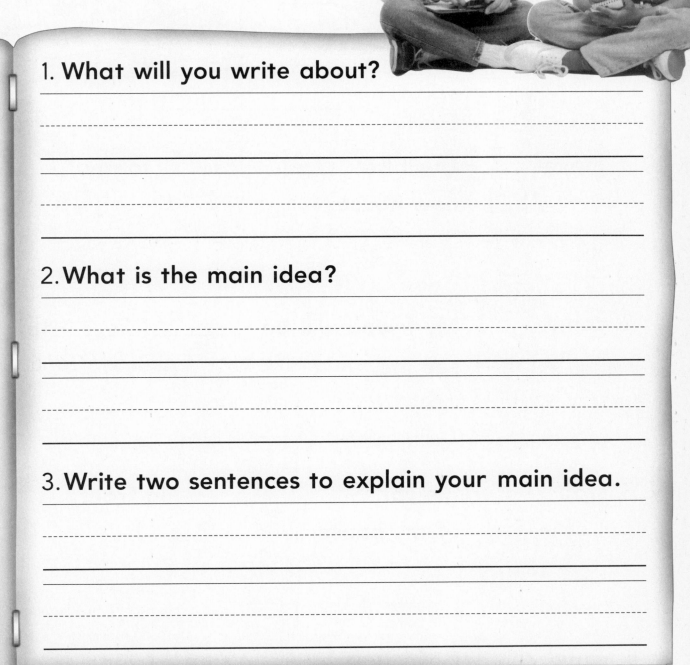

1. **What will you write about?**

   _____

   _____

   _____

2. **What is the main idea?**

   _____

   _____

   _____

3. **Write two sentences to explain your main idea.**

   _____

   _____

   _____

Name _____

A Good Move

Add **-ed** or **-ing** to each base word to
correctly complete the sentence beside it.

1. move   I will be _____ to my
                 new house.

2. come   My friend will be _____ to
                 see me.

3. stop   His car _____ in front
                 of my house.

4. wave   I _____ to my friend.

Name _____

Words to Know

Write a word from the box to complete each sentence.

Word Bank

| put | work | carry | were | person |

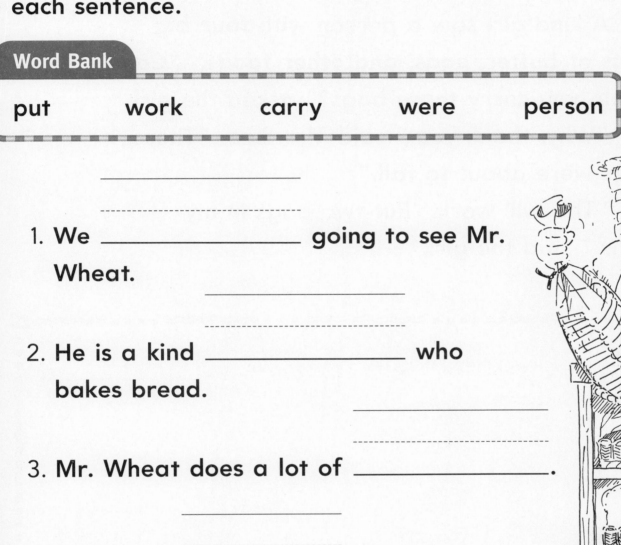

_____

1. We _____ going to see Mr. Wheat.

_____

2. He is a kind _____ who bakes bread.

_____

3. Mr. Wheat does a lot of _____.

_____

4. I saw him _____ butter on a loaf.

_____

5. "You can _____ this home," he said.

Name _____

Words to Know

 Read the story. Draw a picture to go with it.

A kind girl saw a person with four big bags of butter, eggs, and other foods. "Can I help you carry those bags?" asked the girl.

"Why, thank you," said Mrs. Lee. "These bags were about to fall."

"This will work. Put two bags in my arms," said the girl.

Gramp's Stories

Circle and write the word that completes each sentence.

1. Many _____ ago, Gramps lived on a ranch.

   parts   years

2. As a young boy, he cleaned his clothes in the _____ .

   river   nest

3. He helped mash apples to make _____.

   work   cider

4. He helped make _____ for meals.

   bread   stories

Name _____

Apples, Apples, Apples

Draw a picture that shows something Johnny Appleseed did.

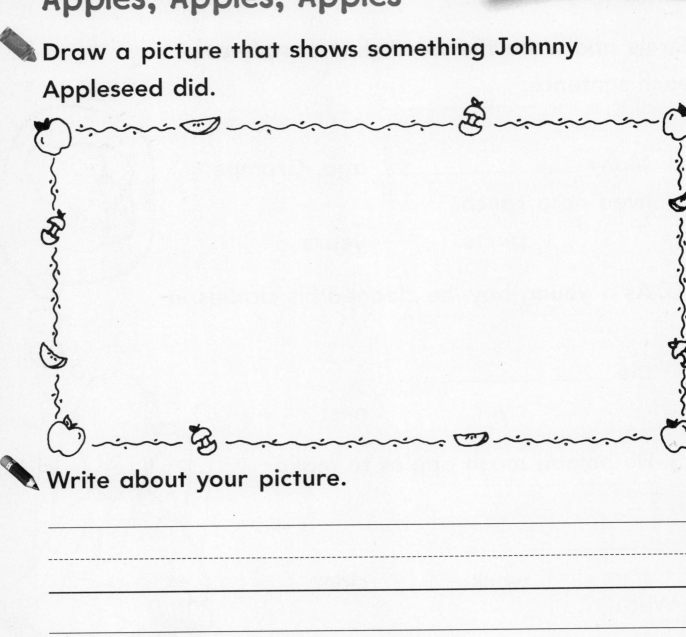

Write about your picture.

_____
- -
_____

_____
- -
_____

_____
- -
_____

Name _____

A New Pet

Read the story and complete the chart.

Dave and Deb wanted a pet. Deb
wanted a dog. Dave wanted a cat.
One day they heard a bark coming
from inside the house.

Conclusion:

_____

- -

_____

Story Clues:

_____

- -

_____

_____

- -

What You Know:

_____

- -

_____

_____

- -

_____

Name _____

Words with *-ed* or *-ing*

Write the correct Spelling Word
under each clue.

Spelling Words

landed
checking
telling
missed
filled
sleeping

1. **looking for something**

   _____

   _____

2. **made something full**

   _____

   _____

3. **not being awake**

   _____

   _____

4. **did not catch**

   _____

   _____

5. **came down to the ground**

   _____

   _____

6. **talking about something**

   _____

   _____

Name _____

Sounds the Same

Complete each sentence with a word from the
box that sounds like the word in dark print.

Word Bank

| new | for | to | eight |

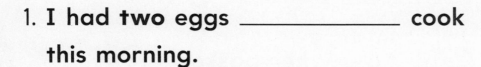

1. I had **two** eggs _____ cook
   this morning.

2. I **ate** _____ eggs for my
   lunch.

3. I had **four** eggs _____ a snack.

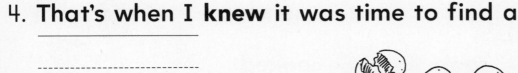

4. That's when I **knew** it was time to find a
   _____ food!

Name _____

Filled It, Spilled It!

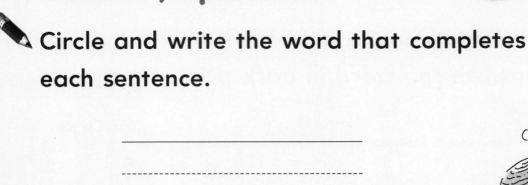

Circle and write the word that completes each sentence.

_____
- -

1. Liz _____ a lot.

          picked   pick

_____
- -

2. She _____ her basket.

          filled   fill

_____
- -

3. Then she _____.

          slipping   slipped

_____
- -

4. So Liz _____ soup.

          cook   cooked

Name _____

Spelling Spree

Write three Spelling Words that end
with **-ed.**

1. _____

2. _____

3. _____

Spelling Words

landed
checking
telling
missed
filled
sleeping

Proofread each sentence. Circle each Spelling
Word that is wrong, and write it correctly.

_____

4. Mom was cheking the bag.   _____

_____

5. She was tellng me to help.   _____

_____

6. I was slepin!   _____

Writing Clearly

Read each sentence. Circle the action word that tells more. Write it on the line.

_____

----

1. Lee _____ a bucket of paint.

   got   grabbed

   _____

   ----

2. The paint _____.

   slipped   fell

   _____

   ----

3. It _____ on Lee's cat.

   went   dripped

   _____

   ----

4. It _____ on Lee's pants.

   got   sprayed

   _____

   ----

5. Paint _____ everywhere!

   splashed   was

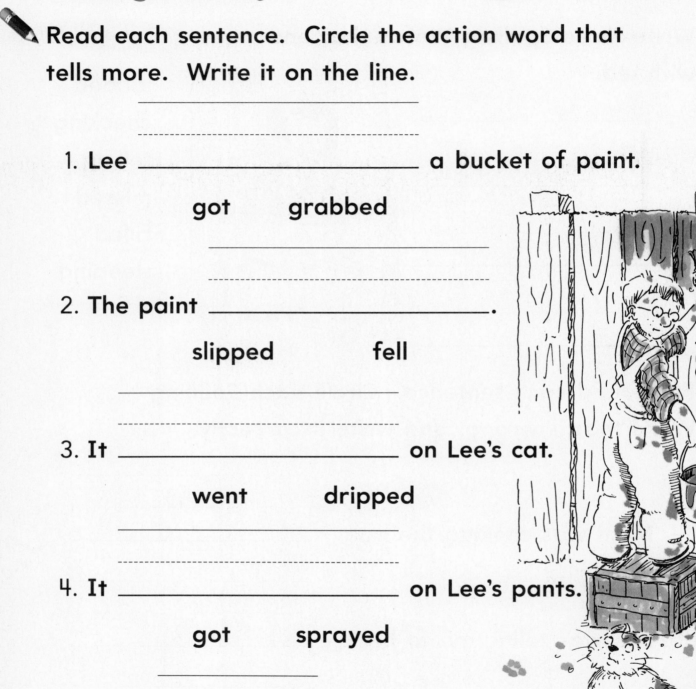

Name _____

Choosing the Best Answer

Now use what you have learned about taking tests. Answer these questions about the story **Johnny Appleseed**. Look back at the story if you need to. This practice will help you when you take this kind of test.

Read each question. Fill in the circle next to the best answer.

1 Why did Johnny Appleseed want to plant apple seeds?

○ He wanted to eat apples.

○ He liked planting seeds.

○ He wanted to make the West a nice place to live.

2 What kind of hat did Johnny Appleseed wear?

○ A cooking pot

○ A cap

○ A rag

Name _____

Choosing the Best Answer

 continued

3 What did Johnny do when it snowed?

○ He stopped.

○ He made snowshoes.

○ He started running.

4 Where did Johnny plant the first apple seed?

○ By an apple tree

○ On a hill

○ By a river

5 How did Johnny feel about wild animals?

○ He was afraid of wild animals.

○ He was not afraid of wild animals.

○ He did not like wild animals.

6 Where did Johnny sleep?

○ On a bed

○ In a house

○ Under the stars

Spelling Review

▲ Add or take off an ending to make each word into a Spelling Word from the box. Write the Spelling Word.

1. tree _____

2. fill _____

3. check _____

4. frogs _____

▲ Write the two Spelling Words that have the vowel sound you hear in **owl**.

5. _____

6. _____

Name _____

Spelling Spree

Write the Spelling Word that rhymes with each word in dark print.

Spelling Words

frog

trees

out

now

sleeping

found

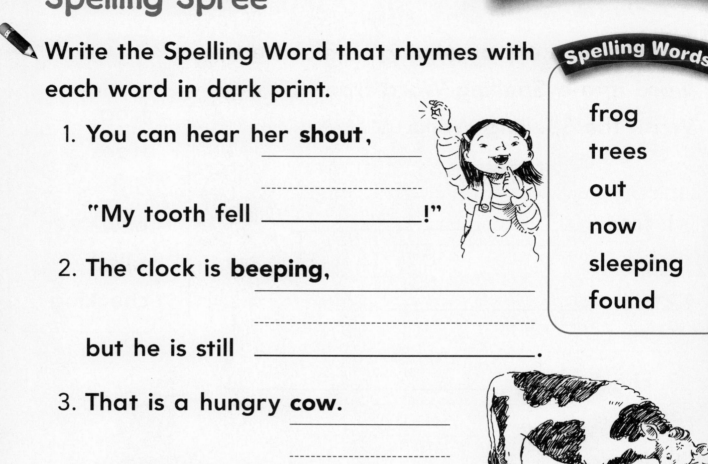

1. You can hear her **shout**,

_____

"My tooth fell _____!"

2. The clock is **beeping**,

_____

but he is still _____.

3. That is a hungry **cow**.

_____

We will feed her _____.

Proofread each sentence. Circle each Spelling Word that is wrong, and write it correctly.

4. Treas can be homes for animals. _____

5. Birds can be fownd in the tops. _____

6. A frogg can live there, too!

Name _____

Words to Know

Circle and write the correct word to complete each sentence.

1. We love to be around the _____.

    though   ocean   else

2. We _____ in the waves.

    ever   dance   though

3. We _____ a box of snacks.

    ocean   around   open

4. Even though it's cool, it's the best _____

    day _____!

    ever   dance   talk

Name _____

Words to Know

 Write the correct word from the box for each clue.

Word Bank

ever	talk	dance	ocean
though	else	around	open

1. Ask someone ____.

2. Means "to speak"

3. Sounds like **never**

4. Means "the sea"

5. Sounds like **go**

6. Not closed

7. We sing and ____.

 Write the letter from each circle.

_____

_____

_____

Name _____

Spelling Spree

Circle and write the hidden Spelling Words.

Spelling Words

by	my	fly	try	cry	why

1. scryth _____

2. scafly _____

3. smylie _____

Proofread each sentence. Circle each Spelling Word that is wrong, and write it correctly.

4. Whie are you crying? _____

5. Come sit bigh me. _____

6. I will tri to help. _____

Theme 9: **Special Friends**   205

Name _____

Story Response

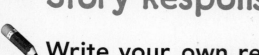 Write your own response to the story
When I Am Old with You.

_____

Title: _____

_____

What did you think of the story?

_____

_____

_____

Would you recommend it to a friend? Why?

_____

_____

_____

Revising Your Friendly Letter

Check the boxes next to the sentences that describe your friendly letter.

Superstar

☐ My letter has all five parts in it.

☐ The parts of my letter are complete.

☐ The body of my letter makes sense.

☐ I wrote interesting details in my letter.

Rising Star

☐ Some parts of my letter are missing or are out of order.

☐ Some parts are not complete.

☐ I need more details to make my letter more interesting.

What's Missing?

 Write each date correctly by adding a
comma. Circle each comma.

1. May 6 1945

_____

_____

2. August 9 2000

_____

_____

3. February 1 1989

_____

_____

4. September 23 2002

_____

_____

Write today's date correctly. Remember to
write the year.

_____

_____

Name _____

Words to Know

Write the correct word from the box for each clue.

after	before	buy	pretty
school	done	off	wash

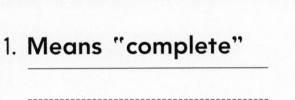

1. Means "complete"

   _____

   _____

2. Not before

   _____

   _____

3. Means "nice to look at"

   _____

   _____

4. Means "to pay for"

   _____

   _____

5. It's a place to learn.

   _____

   _____

6. Means "to clean"

   _____

   _____

7. Not on

   _____

   _____

8. Not after

   _____

   _____

Name _____

Words to Know

 Read each sentence. Draw a picture to go with it.

After school today, my dad is taking me to buy the pretty dress we saw in the shop.

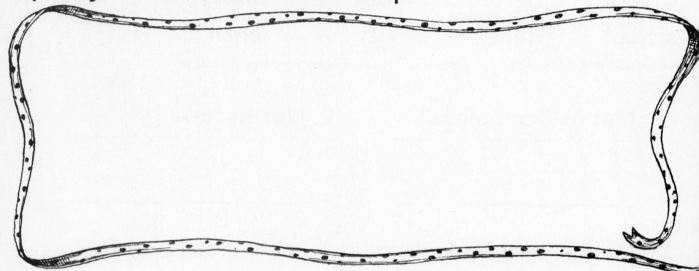

When I am done making cookies, I will wash off the table before lunch.

Name _____

Come to a Party!

Read the invitation.

> ### Come to a Birthday Party!
>
> **Place:** Seventh City Soccer Club
>
> **When:** May 7, 2002
>
> We'll have lots of cookies and
> cake to fill your empty tummy!
>
> This will be the best party in years!

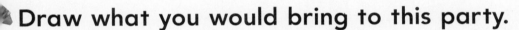

Draw what you would bring to this party.

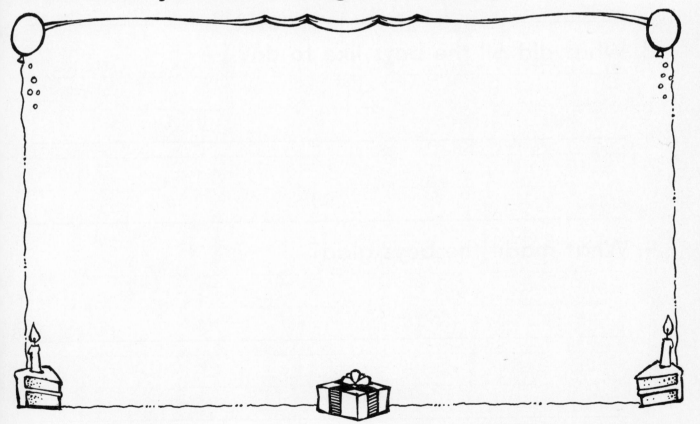

Name _____

What Happened?

Answer the questions to tell what happened in the story.

1. **Who moved into the empty house?**

   _____

   _____

   _____

2. **Where was Makoto from?**

   _____

   _____

3. **What did all the boys like to do?**

   _____

   _____

   _____

4. **What made the boys glad?**

   _____

   _____

   _____

Spelling Spree

Write the two Spelling Words that rhyme.

Spelling Words

dishes	dresses	boxes
beaches	wishes	kisses

1. _____   2. _____

Proofread each sentence. Circle the Spelling Word
that is wrong, and write it correctly.

_____

3. Fred dreses in trunks.   _____

_____

4. He gets boxs.   _____

_____

5. He kissis Mom.   _____

_____

6. Fred's off to the beashes. _____

Name _____

Finish Them Up

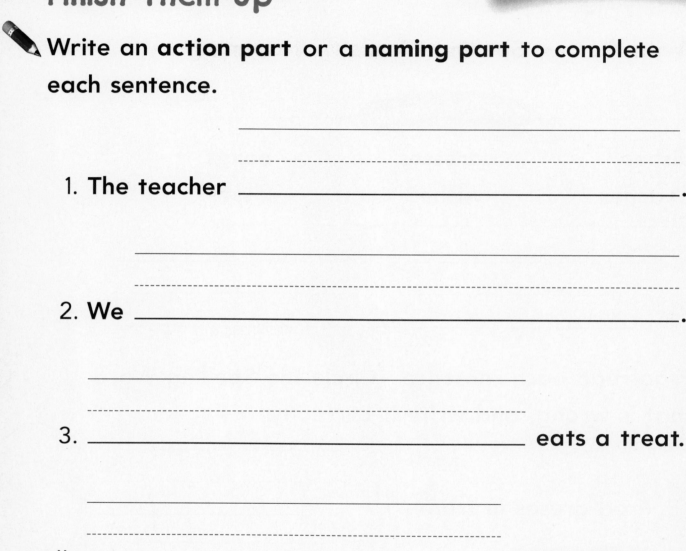

Write an **action part** or a **naming part** to complete each sentence.

1. The teacher _____ .

2. We _____ .

3. _____ eats a treat.

4. _____ finds a flower.

Words to Know

Read the story. Draw a picture to go with it.

We worked together in the garden. The baby watched us work. I used a garden tool with sharp points. We had only a small garden, so we had enough flower seeds to plant. We put pretty flowers around the edge of our garden.

Name _____

Our Chickens

 Write words from the box to complete
the story.

Word Bank

gathered   built   taught   danger   feathers

_____

_____

I _____ my chickens a henhouse. Then

I _____ them to sleep in it. When they

expected to be fed, they _____

at the door. They ate grit for their gizzards. Then

they fluffed their _____ .

When they saw the vacuum cleaner, they squawked,

"Awwk!" It was their _____ cry.

Name _____

The Vowel Sound in *coin*

▲ Use the letter for each shape to write
two Spelling Words.

coin

soil

boy

oil

toy

point

1. _____   2. _____

▲ Write the Spelling Word that goes with each picture.

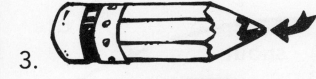

3. _____

4. _____

5. _____

6. _____

Puzzle Fun

 Find the shapes with words that show ownership. Color then orange.

 Then complete the sentences below.

1. If this pet belongs to a girl, it is _____ pet.

2. If this pet belongs to a boy, it is _____ pet.

Name _____

Writing an Answer to a Question continued

✎ Write your answer to each question.

1 What kind of mother do you think the chick expected? Why?

_____
_____
_____
_____
_____
_____
_____

2 What does the boy do for the chick?

_____
_____
_____
_____
_____
_____

Name _____

Spelling Review

 Add **es** to each word to spell a word from the box. Write each word.

Spelling Words

cry

boxes

wishes

boy

dresses

coin

_____

1. dress _____

_____

2. box _____

_____

3. wish _____

Write the two Spelling Words that have the vowel sound you hear in **oink**.

_____

4. _____

_____

5. _____

Write the Spelling Word that you have not used.

_____

6. _____

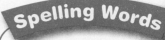

Name _____

Spelling Spree

Write the Spelling Word that completes each sentence.

point

try

boy

wishes

fly

beaches

1. The _____ plays with the baby.

2. She will _____ to get the kite.

3. One crayon has a sharp _____.

Proofread each sentence. Circle each Spelling Word that is wrong, and write it correctly.

_____

4. I would like two wishs.

_____

_____

5. I want to fli like a bird.

_____

_____

6. I want to go over beachs.   _____

Name _____

Word Store

Read the word at the top of the store. Read the directions, and write the new words. The starred one is done for you.

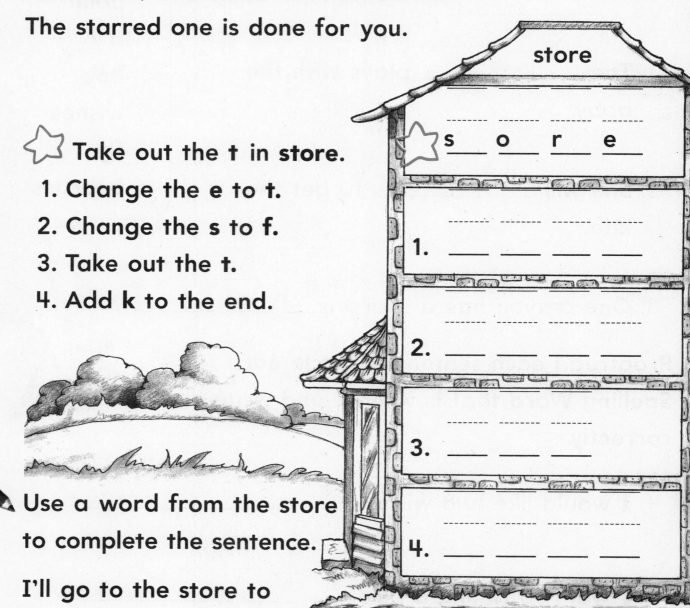

store

☆ Take out the **t** in **store**.

1. Change the **e** to **t**.

2. Change the **s** to **f**.

3. Take out the **t**.

4. Add **k** to the end.

☆ s o r e

1. _____

2. _____

3. _____

4. _____

Use a word from the store to complete the sentence.

I'll go to the store to

_____

look _____ some more forks.

Name _____

A Full Day

Read the story below. Write each word in dark print below the picture it names.

Jill rides a **horse**. Sam goes to the **store**. Mort plays the **horn**. Norm plants some **corn**. Others play **sports**. Nan keeps **score**. No one is bored!

1.

_____

_____

2.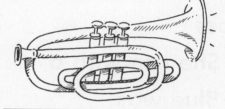

_____

_____

3.

_____

_____

4.

_____

_____

5.

_____

_____

6.

_____

_____

Jo's Home Run

 Finish each sentence with a word from the Word Bank.
Write each word in the correct puzzle boxes.

Word Bank

turn   girl   burst   shirt   her   third

Across

1. She ran with a _____ of speed.

2. Blue was _____ team's color.

3. Jo hit the ball past _____ base.

Down

4. Jo wore a blue _____ .

5. It was Jo's _____ at bat.

6. That _____ hit a home run!

What Will Gert Wear?

Circle and write the word that completes each sentence.

_____
- - - - - - - - - - - - - - - - - - -

1. Gert looks at _____ three shirts.

    horse   her   fur

_____
- - - - - - - - - - - - - - - - - - -

2. Her _____ is too small.

    shirt   sir   shore

_____
- - - - - - - - - - - - - - - - - - -

3. This shirt is too _____ .

    day   curly   dirty

_____
- - - - - - - - - - - - - - - - - - -

4. Here's her _____ shirt.

    stir   third   turn

_____
- - - - - - - - - - - - - - - - - - -

5. This shirt is _____ !

    perfect   germ   bird

Name _____

Words to Know

 Read each story. Draw a picture to go with it.

I can't break that candy in two. You give it a try, and I'll give it a second try. We sure can divide candy!

Jeff began to tell a joke. I began to laugh. I laughed until my head hurt!

Name _____

Words to Know

Fold a piece of paper in half to make a book.

Cut out and paste the story parts on the pages in order.

Write your own ending on the last page.

A Better Idea

Buzz and Fuzz found a log.

"Let's divide it with an ax," said Buzz.

"I'm sure that will work."

"We have these big teeth!" said Fuzz.

"We can chew the log in two!"

Buzz laughed, too. "Sure!" he said.

They hit the log. It didn't break.

They tried a second time. Buzz

shook his head. Fuzz began

to laugh.

Whole or Half?

Write a word from the box to complete each sentence.

Word Bank

divide	equal	whole	half	halves

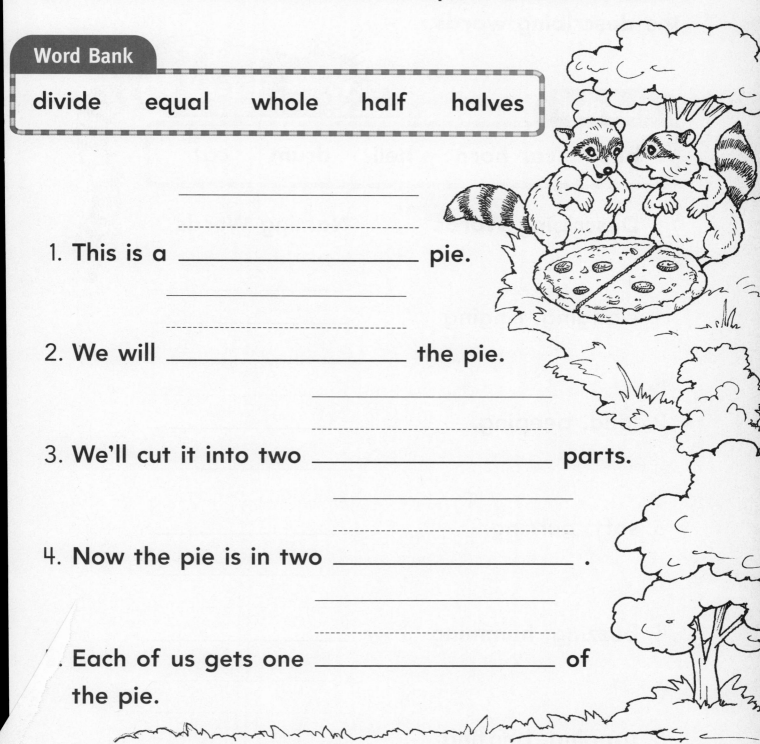

1. This is a _____ pie.

2. We will _____ the pie.

3. We'll cut it into two _____ parts.

4. Now the pie is in two _____ .

_. Each of us gets one _____ of the pie.

Sound Match

Write **naming words** from the box that match
the **describing words.**

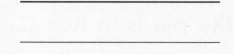

Word Bank

| bee | car horn | bell | drum | cat |

Describing Words	Naming Words

1. clanging, ringing _____

2. loud, beeping _____

3. soft, purring _____

4. buzzing, humming _____

5. tapping, beating _____

Name _____

Revising Your Instructions

✎ Check the sentences that tell about your writing.

Superstar

☐ I have a good beginning sentence.

☐ My instructions are in 1-2-3 order.

☐ I used time-order words.

☐ I wrote about something I know how to do well and can explain clearly.

☐ My instructions are easy to follow and interesting to read.

Rising Star

☐ I need to put my instructions in 1-2-3 order.

☐ I need to add time-order words.

☐ I need to explain this better.

Name _____

Writing Clear Sentences

Make sentences. Write each group of words in the correct order. Add a period at the end of the sentence.

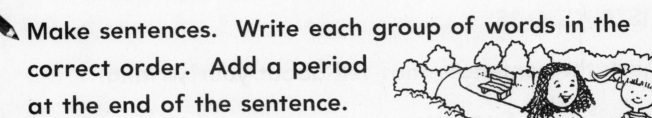

1. park   to   We   the   went

_____

- -

_____

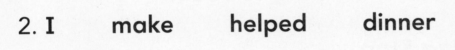

2. I   make   helped   dinner

_____

- -

_____

3. new   She   shoes   got

_____

- -

_____

Words to Know

Read each pair of sentences. Circle the
sentence that goes with the picture.

The baby will begin to walk soon.
The puppy can already walk.

A bird is flying above the tree.
A boy is leaning against the tree.

Jack has just caught his bus.
Jill must wait one more minute.

Name _____

Words to Know

Read each question. Write the word in dark print that answers it.

1. Is Bear **above** the wall or **against** the wall?

_____

_____

2. Which is longer: one **second** or one **minute?**

_____

_____

3. Which word means to start: **begin** or **end?**

_____

_____

Circle the picture that answers each question.

4. Who **caught** the ball?

5. Which flower is **already** blooming?

Name _____

Carl's Journey

Circle and write the word that completes each sentence.

1. Carl is going on a space _____ .

   beacon   journey

2. People _____ to wish him luck.

   appear   whispers

3. "Follow the beacon of light," _____ Andy.

   appears   warns

4. Carl _____ to take pictures.

   promises   beacons

5. This journey is Carl's _____ .

   monarch   favorite

Proud of My Sister

Circle the word that makes sense in each sentence.

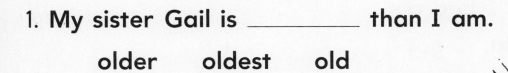

1. My sister Gail is _____ than I am.

    older   oldest   old

2. We are the _____ sisters I know.

    close   closer   closest

3. Gail is the _____ runner in our school.

    fasting   fastest   faster

4. She can also run _____ than anyone.

    longer   longing   longest

5. She is the _____ person to beat.

    hardly   harder   hardest

6. I am the _____ sister around!

    proudest   proud   proudly

Name _____

Words to Know

Read the story.

I was able to run to the store today. I had a smart thought. I got you a present. Close one eye at a time.

What do you think the present is? Draw and write your answer.

_____

_____

_____

_____

_____

Name _____

Words to Know

Finish each sentence with a word from the Word Bank. Write each word in the correct puzzle boxes.

Word Bank

able   eye   present   thought

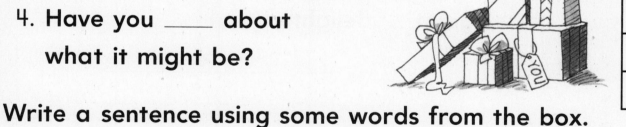

Across

1. We were ____ to go to the party after all.
2. That ____ is for you.

Down

3. Keep one ____ on the present.
4. Have you ____ about what it might be?

Write a sentence using some words from the box.

_____

_____

_____

Name _____

A Present from Ed

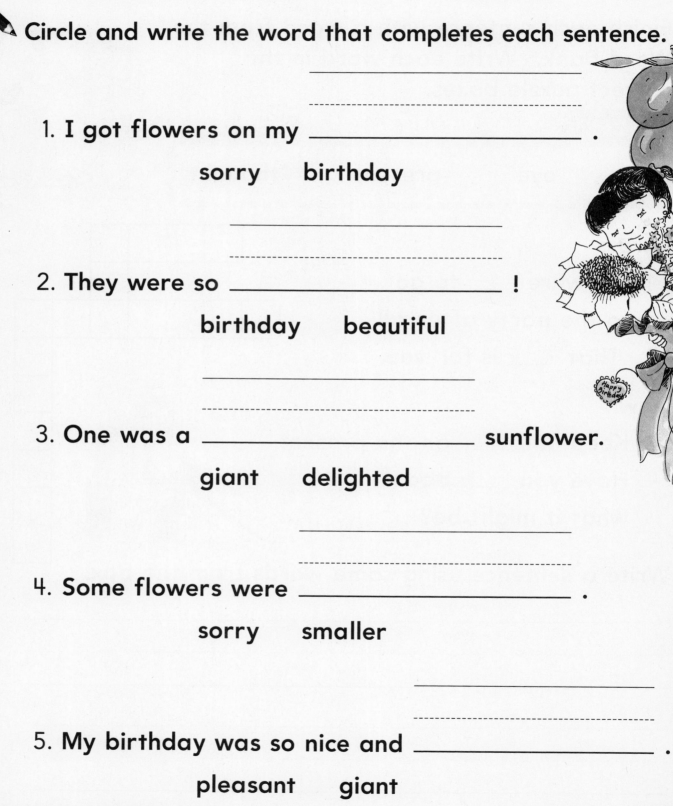

Circle and write the word that completes each sentence.

_____

1. I got flowers on my _____ .

   sorry   birthday

_____

2. They were so _____ !

   birthday   beautiful

_____

3. One was a _____ sunflower.

   giant   delighted

_____

4. Some flowers were _____ .

   sorry   smaller

_____

5. My birthday was so nice and _____ .

   pleasant   giant

Name _____

Adding *er* and *est* to Words

✏ Write a Spelling Word from the box to complete each sentence.

_____

1. Today is the _____ day of the summer.

_____

2. This pool is _____ than the old one in town.

_____

3. Otter swam _____ than anyone else.

_____

4. Now Otter is at the _____ spot.

_____

5. Otter dove into the _____ water.

_____

6. Otter feels _____ than a king!

Name _____

How Do They Do It?

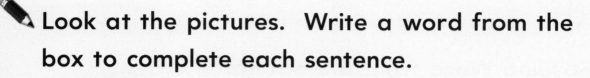 Look at the pictures. Write a word from the box to complete each sentence.

Word Bank

| tightly | kindly | quickly | loudly | slowly |

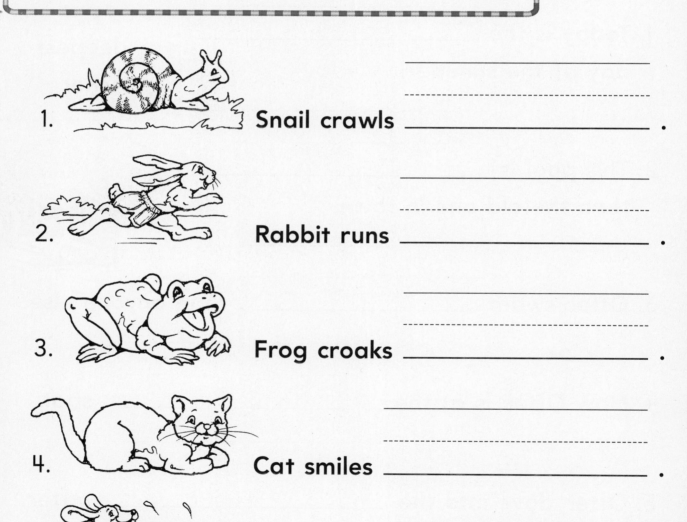

1. Snail crawls _____ .

2. Rabbit runs _____ .

3. Frog croaks _____ .

4. Cat smiles _____ .

5. Dog holds on _____ .

Name _____

Writing a Personal Narrative

Use what you have learned about taking tests. First, make a chart to help you plan. Next, write your narrative. Then see how you can make your answer better.

In **Two Greedy Bears,** the bear cubs learn that arguing doesn't always solve their problems. Write about a time when you solved a problem without arguing.

_____
- -
_____
_____
- -
_____
_____
- -
_____
_____
- -
_____
_____
- -
_____

Name _____

Writing a Personal Narrative

continued

Read your personal narrative. Check off each box that tells about your answer.

- [ ] The beginning tells what my narrative is about.
- [ ] My narrative has the words **I** and **me**.
- [ ] My narrative has details that help the reader picture what happened.
- [ ] The ending tells how I felt.

If you did not check a box, you can make your answer better. Make your changes here.

_____

_____

_____

_____

_____

_____

_____

My Handbook

Contents

Andy Apple

Benny Bear

Callie Cat

Dudley Duck

Edna Elephant

Fifi Fish

Gertie Goose

Hattie Horse

Iggy Iguana

Jumping Jill

Keely Kangaroo

Larry Lion

Mimi Mouse

Nyle Noodle

Ozzie Octopus

Pippa Pig

Queenie Queen

Reggie Rooster

Sammy Seal

Tiggy Tiger

Umbie Umbrella

Vinny Volcano

Willy Worm

Mr. X-Ray

Yetta Yo-Yo

Zelda Zebra

1. **Look at the letters from left to right.**

2. **Think about the sounds for the letters, and look for word parts you know.**

3. **Blend the sounds to read the word.**

4. Ask yourself: **Is it a word I know? Does it make sense in what I am reading?**

5. If not, ask yourself: **What else can I try?**

Predict/Infer

► Think about the title, the illustrations, and what you have read so far.

► Tell what you think will happen next or what you will learn.

Question

► Ask yourself questions as you read.

Monitor/Clarify

► Ask yourself if what you are reading makes sense.

► If you don't understand something, reread, read ahead, or use the illustrations.

Summarize

► Think about the main ideas or the important parts of the story.

► Tell the important things in your own words.

Evaluate

► Ask yourself: Do I like what I have read? Am I learning what I wanted to know?

Writing the Alphabet

Trace and write the letters.

Aa *Aa*

Bb *Bb*

Cc *Cc*

Dd *Dd*

Ee *Ee*

Ff *Ff*

Gg *Gg*

Trace and write the letters.

Hh Hh

Ii Ii

Jj Jj

Kk Kk

Ll Ll

Mm Mm

Trace and write the letters.

Nn Nn

Oo Oo

Pp Pp

Qq Qq

Rr Rr

Ss Ss

Tt Tt

✎ **Trace and write the letters.**

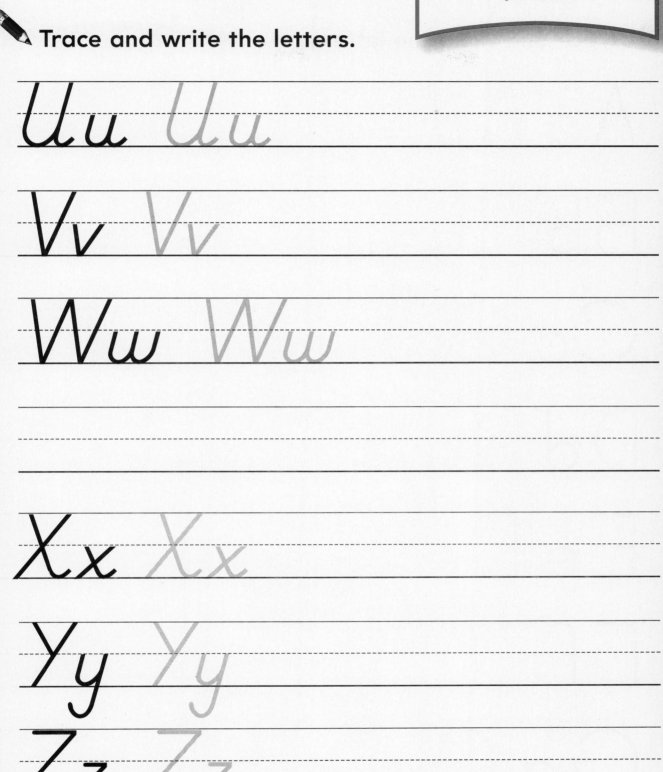

Uu Uu

Vv Vv

Ww Ww

Xx Xx

Yy Yy

Zz Zz

Trace and write the letters.

A a A a

B b B b

C c C c

D d D d

E e E e

F f F f

G g G g

Trace and write the letters.

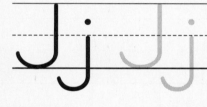

Trace and write the letters.

Nn Nn

Oo Oo

Pp Pp

Qq Qq

Rr Rr

Ss Ss

Tt Tt

Trace and write the letters.

U u U u

V v V v

W w W w

X x X x

Y y Y y

Z z Z z

How to Study a Word

1. **LOOK** at the word.

2. **SAY** the word.

3. **THINK** about the word.

4. **WRITE** the word.

5. **CHECK** the spelling.

A

a
about
again
all
always
and
any
around
as

B

back
because
before

C

cannot
come
coming
could

D

do
down

F

for
friend
from

G

getting
goes
going

H

has
have
her
here
his
house
how

I

I
if
into
is

L

little

M

many
more

N

never
new
now

O

of

one

or

other

our

out

over

P

people

R

right

S

said

some

T

than

the

their

there

they

thing

to

tried

two

V

very

W

want

was

were

what

when

where

who

would

Y

you

your

Me on the Map

The Long *a* Sound

make

came

take

Spelling Words

1. make
2. came
3. take
4. name
5. gave
6. game

Challenge Words

1. place
2. skate

My Study List
Add your own spelling words on the back. ➡

Moving Day

Words Spelled with *sh* or *ch*

she   chin

fish   much

Spelling Words

1. she
2. chin
3. fish
4. shell
5. much
6. chop

Challenge Words

1. shoe
2. chair

My Study List
Add your own spelling words on the back. ➡

Take-Home Word List

Name _____

My Study List

_____

1. _____

2. _____

3. _____

4. _____

5. _____

6. _____

Name _____

My Study List

_____

1. _____

2. _____

3. _____

4. _____

5. _____

6. _____

Home Sweet Home
Spelling Review

Spelling Words

1. shell
2. make
3. like
4. fish
5. gave
6. kite
7. ride
8. chop
9. name
10. much

See the back for Challenge Words.

My Study List
Add your own spelling words on the back. ➡

The Kite

The Long *i* Sound
like
five

Spelling Words

1. like
2. five
3. ride
4. nine
5. time
6. kite

Challenge Words

1. prize
2. smile

My Study List
Add your own spelling words on the back. ➡

Name_____

My Study List

_____

1. _____

2. _____

3. _____

4. _____

5. _____

6. _____

Name_____

My Study List

_____

1. _____

2. _____

3. _____

4. _____

5. _____

6. _____

Challenge Words

1. chair
2. place
3. prize

EEK! There's a Mouse in the House

The Long *e* Sound

me

see

mean

Spelling Words

1. me
2. see
3. mean
4. feet
5. eat
6. he

Challenge Words

1. maybe
2. sheep

My Study List
Add your own spelling words on the back. ➡

The Sleeping Pig

The Long *o* Sound

go

bone

nose

Spelling Words

1. go
2. bone
3. so
4. nose
5. home
6. no

Challenge Words

1. also
2. woke

My Study List
Add your own spelling words on the back. ➡

Name_____

My Study List

_____

1. _____

2. _____

3. _____

4. _____

5. _____

6. _____

Name_____

My Study List

_____

1. _____

2. _____

3. _____

4. _____

5. _____

6. _____

Animal Adventures
Spelling Review

Spelling Words

1. go
2. me
3. day
4. feet
5. nose
6. eat
7. play
8. mean
9. home
10. stay

See the back for Challenge Words.

My Study List
Add your own spelling words on the back. ➡

Red-Eyed Tree Frog

The Long _a_ Sound Spelled _ay_

day   say

play

Spelling Words

1. day
2. say
3. play
4. may
5. way
6. stay

Challenge Words

1. away
2. holiday

My Study List
Add your own spelling words on the back. ➡

Name_____

My Study List

1. _____

2. _____

3. _____

4. _____

5. _____

6. _____

Take-Home Word List

Name_____

My Study List

1. _____

2. _____

3. _____

4. _____

5. _____

6. _____

Challenge Words

1. woke

2. sheep

3. away

Lost!

The Vowel Sound in
book

look   foot
good

Spelling Words

1. look
2. book
3. took
4. good
5. foot
6. cook

Challenge Words

1. hoof
2. crook

My Study List
Add your own
spelling words
on the back. ➡

That Toad Is Mine!

More Long *o* Spellings
boat   slow
coat   grow

Spelling Words

1. boat
2. slow
3. coat
4. grow
5. show
6. toad

Challenge Words

1. coast
2. know

My Study List
Add your own
spelling words
on the back. ➡

Name_____

My Study List

1. _____

2. _____

3. _____

4. _____

5. _____

6. _____

Name_____

My Study List

1. _____

2. _____

3. _____

4. _____

5. _____

6. _____

We Can Work It Out
Spelling Review

Spelling Words

1. toad
2. look
3. good
4. grow
5. book
6. too
7. zoo
8. show
9. moon
10. coat

See the back for Challenge Words.

My Study List
Add your own spelling words on the back. ➡️

If You Give a Pig a Pancake

The Vowel Sound in _moon_

zoo   soon
food

Spelling Words

1. zoo
2. food
3. too
4. moon
5. soon
6. room

Challenge Words

1. moose
2. balloon

My Study List
Add your own spelling words on the back. ➡️

Name _____

My Study List

_____

1. _____

2. _____

3. _____

4. _____

5. _____

6. _____

Name _____

My Study List

_____

1. _____

2. _____

3. _____

4. _____

5. _____

6. _____

Challenge Words

1. know
2. hoof
3. moose

Butterfly

The Forest

The Vowel Sound in *cow*

house   down

out   now

Adding *s* **to Naming Words**

cups

trees

Spelling Words

1. cow
2. house
3. out
4. down
5. now
6. found

Spelling Words

1. cup
2. cups
3. frog
4. frogs
5. tree
6. trees

Challenge Words

1. pouch
2. crowded

Challenge Words

1. gloves
2. birds

My Study List
Add your own
spelling words
on the back. ➡

My Study List
Add your own
spelling words
on the back. ➡

Name_____

My Study List

_____

1. _____

2. _____

3. _____

4. _____

5. _____

6. _____

Name_____

My Study List

_____

1. _____

2. _____

3. _____

4. _____

5. _____

6. _____

The New Friend

Adding *es* to Naming Words

| dishes | boxes |
| dresses | beaches |

Spelling Words

1. dishes
2. dresses
3. boxes
4. beaches
5. wishes
6. kisses

Challenge Words

1. classes
2. brushes

My Study List
Add your own spelling words on the back. ➡

When I Am Old with You

The Long *i* Sound Spelled *y*

| by | fly |
| try | |

Spelling Words

1. by
2. my
3. fly
4. try
5. cry
6. why

Challenge Words

1. pry
2. multiply

My Study List
Add your own spelling words on the back. ➡

Name _____

My Study List

_____
- - - - - - - - - - - - - - - - - -

1. _____
   _____
- - - - - - - - - - - - - - - - - -

2. _____
   _____
- - - - - - - - - - - - - - - - - -

3. _____
   _____
- - - - - - - - - - - - - - - - - -

4. _____
   _____
- - - - - - - - - - - - - - - - - -

5. _____
   _____
- - - - - - - - - - - - - - - - - -

6. _____

Name _____

My Study List

_____
- - - - - - - - - - - - - - - - - -

1. _____
   _____
- - - - - - - - - - - - - - - - - -

2. _____
   _____
- - - - - - - - - - - - - - - - - -

3. _____
   _____
- - - - - - - - - - - - - - - - - -

4. _____
   _____
- - - - - - - - - - - - - - - - - -

5. _____
   _____
- - - - - - - - - - - - - - - - - -

6. _____

Special Friends
Spelling Review

Spelling Words

1. cry
2. boxes
3. boy
4. try
5. wishes
6. dresses
7. point
8. fly
9. beaches
10. coin

See the back for Challenge Words.

My Study List
Add your own spelling words on the back. ➡

The Surprise Family

The Vowel Sound in *coin*

soil   boy

point

Spelling Words

1. coin
2. soil
3. boy
4. oil
5. toy
6. point

Challenge Words

1. moist
2. destroy

My Study List
Add your own spelling words on the back. ➡

Name _____

My Study List

1. _____

2. _____

3. _____

4. _____

5. _____

6. _____

Name _____

My Study List

1. _____

2. _____

3. _____

4. _____

5. _____

6. _____

Challenge Words

1. multiply
2. brushes
3. moist

Fireflies for Nathan

> **The Vowel + *r* Sound in *car***
>
> far   start
> arm

Spelling Words

1. car
2. start
3. arm
4. far
5. yard
6. dark

Challenge Words

1. large
2. jar

My Study List
Add your own
spelling words
on the back. ➡

Two Greedy Bears

> **The Vowel + *r* Sound in *store***
>
> corn   more
> for

Spelling Words

1. store
2. corn
3. for
4. more
5. or
6. morning

Challenge Words

1. afford
2. before

My Study List
Add your own
spelling words
on the back. ➡

Name

My Study List

1.

2.

3.

4.

5.

6.

Name

My Study List

1.

2.

3.

4.

5.

6.

We Can Do It!
Spelling Review

Spelling Words

1. more
2. newer
3. dark
4. warmest
5. morning
6. highest
7. yard
8. corn
9. faster
10. arm

See the back for Challenge Words.

My Study List
Add your own spelling words on the back. ➡

The Hat

Adding *er* or *est* to Words

newer	warmest
faster	highest

Spelling Words

1. newer
2. warmest
3. highest
4. faster
5. deepest
6. richer

Challenge Words

1. smaller
2. kindest

My Study List
Add your own spelling words on the back. ➡

Name _____

My Study List

_____

1. _____

2. _____

3. _____

4. _____

5. _____

6. _____

Name _____

My Study List

_____

1. _____

2. _____

3. _____

4. _____

5. _____

6. _____

Challenge Words

1. afford
2. jar
3. smaller

Answer these questions when you check
your writing.

☐ **Did I begin each sentence with
a capital letter?**

☐ **Did I use the right mark at the end of each
sentence? (. ?)**

☐ **Did I spell each word correctly?**

Proofreading Marks		
⋀	Add	My aunt came ^to^ visit.
——	Take out	We ~~were~~ sang songs.

A A A B B C C D D

E E E F F G G H H

I I J J K K L L M

M N N O O P P Q Q

R R S S T T U U V

V W W X X Y Y Z Z

u can add punctuation marks or other letters to the blanks.

Letter Tray

↓

d	d	c	c	b	b	a	a	a
h	h	g	g	f	f	e	e	e
m	l	l	k	k	j	j	i	i
q	q	p	p	o	o	n	n	m
v	u	u	t	t	s	s	r	r
z	z	y	y	x	x	w	w	v

fold

fold

Theme 5, Week 3	Theme 5, Week 2	Theme 5, Week 1
give	could	grow
good	house	light
her	how	long
little	over	more
try	own	other
was	so	right
fly	world	room
our		these
		small

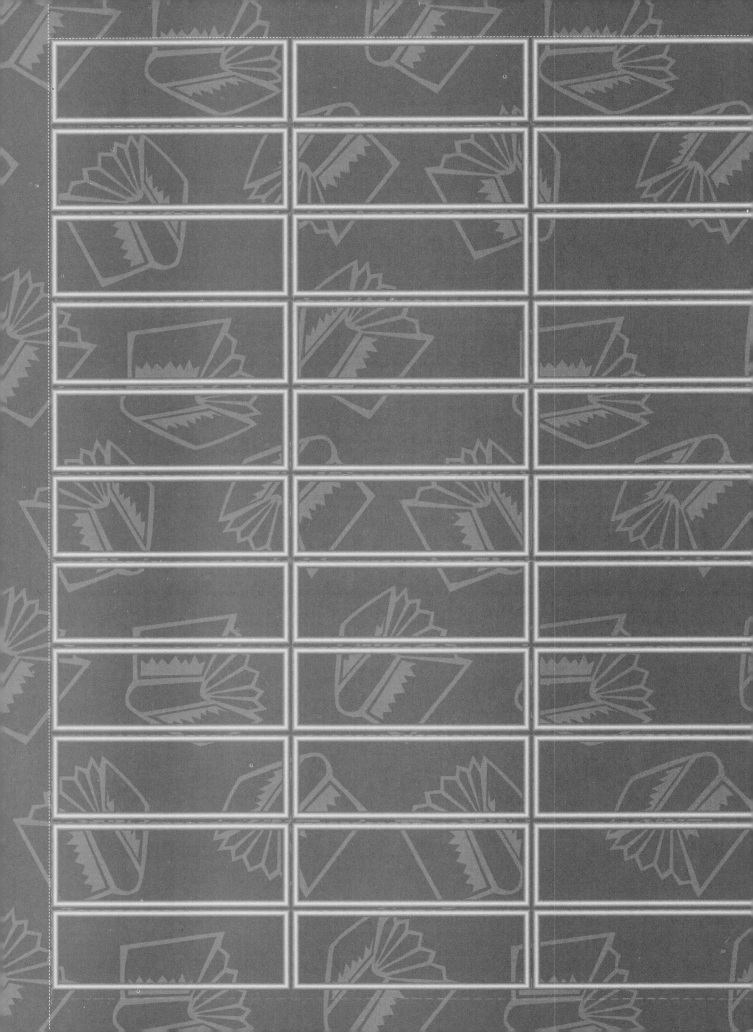

Theme 6, Week 3	Theme 6, Week 2	Theme 6, Week 1
been	cow	morning
far	table	found
forest	now	shout
goes	door	by
hungry	there	out
soon	through	show
evening	horse	climb
near	wall	

can add your own words for sentence building.

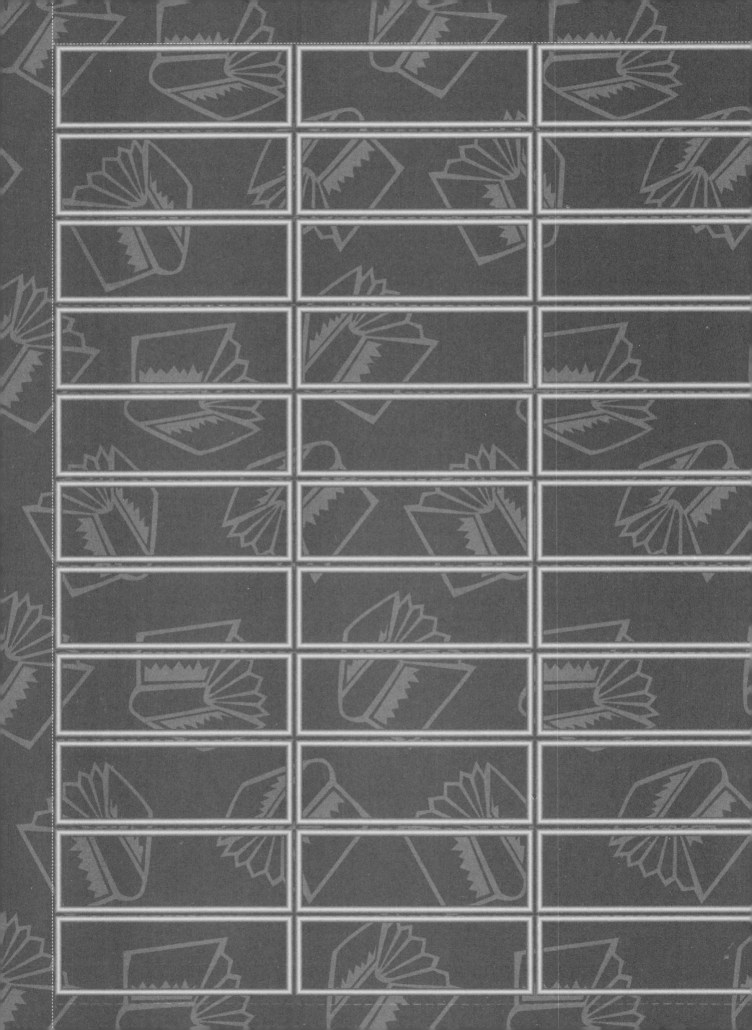

Theme 7, Week 3	Theme 7, Week 2	Theme 7, Week 1
old	afraid	again
piece	any	both
shoe	bear	gone
start	follow	or
under	most	want
very	tall	turn
wear	water	hard
build	idea	

You can add your own words for sentence building.

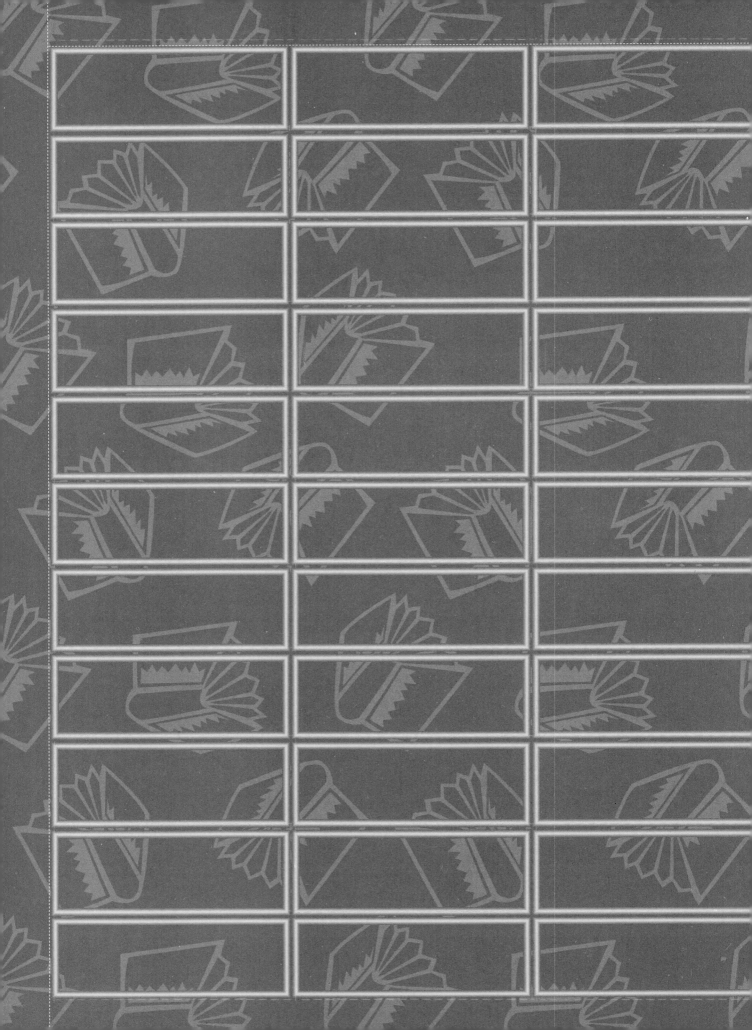

Theme 8, Week 3	Theme 8, Week 2	Theme 8, Week 1
carry	always	about
kind	eight	because
put	arms	draw
saw	seven	happy
butter	warm	teacher
were	ready	part
work	body	tiny
person		

You can add your own words for sentence building.

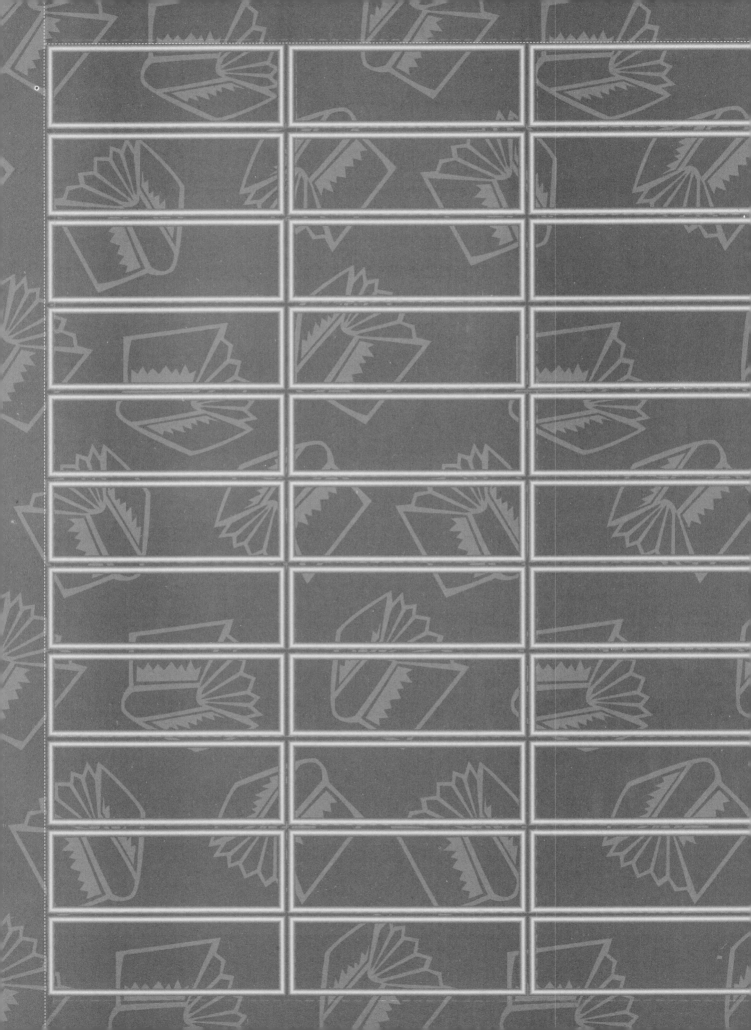

Theme 9, Week 3	Theme 9, Week 2	Theme 9, Week 1
only	after	around
together	before	dance
watched	buy	else
baby	pretty	open
edge	school	talk
enough	done	ever
garden	off	though
sharp	wash	ocean

u can add your own words for sentence building.

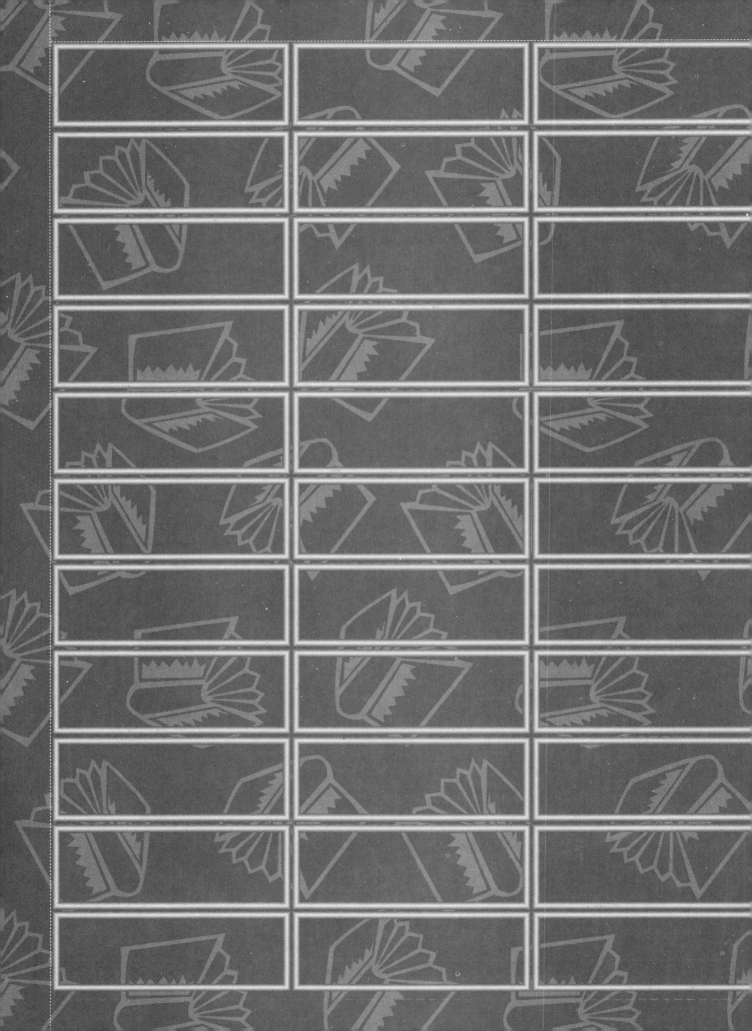

Theme 10, Week 3	Theme 10, Week 2	Theme 10, Week 1
able	above	began
eye	against	laugh
present	already	sure
thoughts	caught	head
	begin	divide
	minute	second
		break

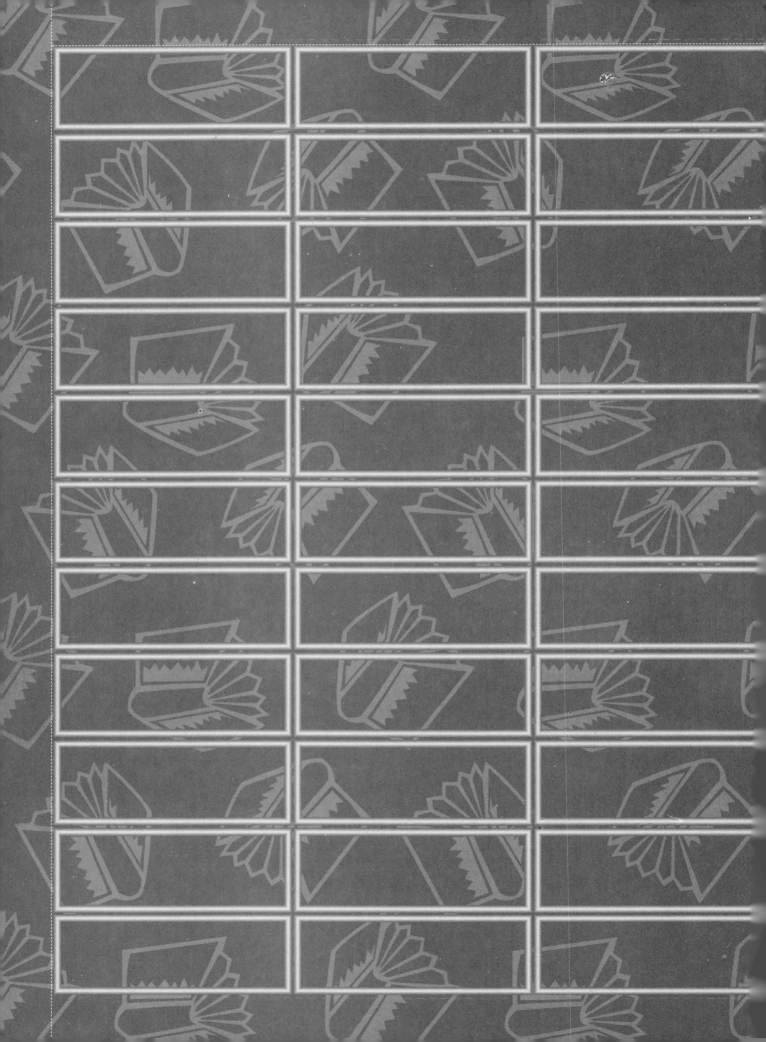